When
Nothing
Makes
Sense

When Nothing Makes Sense

Disaster, Crisis, and Their Effects on Children

Gerald Deskin, Ph.D., M.F.C.C.
Greg Steckler, M.A., M.F.C.C.

Published by Fairview Press, 2450 Riverside Avenue South, Minneapolis, MN 55454.

Alternative Cataloging-in-Publication Data

Deskin, Gerald.
    When nothing makes sense: disaster, crisis, and their effects on children. By Gerald Deskin and Greg Steckler. Minneapolis, MN: Fairview Press, copyright 1996.
    PARTIAL CONTENTS: Children's emotional reaction to crisis. -What to do before a disaster. -True stories. -Mental, emotional, and physical reactions to disaster. -Special family problems after a disaster. -Cultural differences in handling stress and disasters.
    APPENDICIES: Materials to purchase at camping or emergency supply stores. -A relaxation tape.
    1. Children and disasters—Psychological aspects. 2. Child disaster victims—Mental health. 3. Parents of disaster victims—Self-help materials. 4. Stress management for children. 5. Emergency planning. 6. Children—Stress. I. Title. II. Title: Disaster crisis, and their effects on children. III. Steckler, Greg. IV. Fairview Press. V. Title: Nothing makes sense.

649.1 or 618.9289

ISBN 0-925190-95-0 : $19.95

First Printing: March 1996

Printed in the United States of America
00 99 98 97 96   7 6 5 4 3 2 1

Jacket design: Circus Design
Photos on back panel of jacket provided by the American Red Cross

Publisher's Note: Fairview Press publishes books and other materials related to the subjects of family and social issues. Its publications, including *When Nothing Makes Sense* do not necessarily reflect the philosophy of Fairview Hospital and Healthcare Services or their treatment programs.

For a free current catalog of Fairview Press titles, please call this toll-free number: 1-800-544-8207.

Contents

Foreword   *vii*

Preface   *xi*

1. Introduction   1
2. Children's Emotional Reaction to Crisis   17
3. What to Do before a Disaster   25
4. True Stories: The Shaking Earth   59
5. What to Do during a Disaster   63
6. Mental, Emotional, and Physical Reactions to Disaster   71
7. True Stories: The Blowing Wind   81
8. What to Do after a Disaster   85
9. Help after a Disaster   99
10. True Stories: The Burning Forest   105
11. Special Family Problems after a Disaster   109
12. Cultural Differences in Handling Stress and Disasters   115
13. True Stories: The Crazy Man   119
14. An Overview of Some Disasters   123
15. The Media's Impact   147
16. The Aftereffects—Years after a Disaster   153

Appendix A. Materials to Purchase at Camping or
     Emergency Supply Stores   161

Appendix B. A Relaxation Tape   163

Bibliography   *169*

Index   *171*

Your Own Disaster Plan   175

Foreword

Disasters are those relatively sudden, chaotic, destructive, painful, and overwhelming disturbances that periodically afflict our communities. Only rarely in history have the affected communities or the families that make up those communities been reasonably prepared to manage the physical and emotional turmoil produced by natural or technological disasters.

Few people believe that a destructive force could strike their community and inflict severe damage. Even if they believe that they may be vulnerable, most people like to believe that they are strong enough or organized enough to handle whatever comes their way. Practically all people underestimate the power of a disaster to overwhelm their resources and their lives. Likewise they typically overestimate their ability to cope with turmoil.

The tenacious denial, the underlying fear that paralyzes action coupled with underestimating a disaster's power or the overestimating of one's abilities can lead to inadequately prepared individuals, families, and communities. The end result is a greater number of injuries, preventable deaths, and long-range emotional distress.

In spite of extensive efforts on the part of the American Red Cross and a variety of local, state, and federal governmental agencies to educate the public and warn them to be prepared for the worst, disaster preparedness remains a largely ignored endeavor on the part of the average person. All too often people ask "What can be done?" only after the tragedy has struck. For many, that question comes far too late. Learning new tasks, such as managing one's family in the aftermath of a disaster, is extraordinarily difficult in the midst of an ongoing crisis. When too much is left to chance or to "crisis learning," there is a much greater potential for things to go wrong. Individuals and families then have a far more difficult time maintaining stability during the crisis and recovering when it is over. Individuals may hurt more, family life becomes disrupted, and children become unnecessary psychological casualties in a tragedy.

The damages sustained by children today can be carried into their futures. Powerful stressors can cause them pain in the present, but—even more likely—will interfere with their future adjustment to life's stressors. Parents have the opportunity, however, to make a difference. They can set the stage for successful coping patterns in their children.

It is a significant challenge for parents to provide all of the education children need to survive in today's complex world. Most understand that they need to prepare their children for some of life's most stressful experiences. They also recognize that no person can be an expert on every topic. People who are not oriented to disaster management, for example, will have a difficult time helping their children adjust to the demands of a disaster. They simply do not have that kind of knowledge. They are in need of a resource to help them to get the job done.

When Nothing Makes Sense is a useful tool that can be used by parents and others who are responsible for the well-being of children to assure that families and individuals are more adequately prepared to manage a disaster experience. It is the kind of book that is useful after the disaster has struck; it is filled with practical, useful information that normalized the terror and confusion encountered during a disaster. It guides parents in their efforts to adapt to extraordinary circumstances. The book helps parents to understand the distress their children may be experiencing during a crisis. It also offers sensible steps they can employ to assist their children in recovering from the distress, which is a consequence of every disaster.

Gerald Deskin and Greg Steckler have written *When Nothing Makes Sense* in a clear, readable style that the average parent can appreciate. It is not a book to be left on the shelf until something happens. Although it will prove to be useful during recovery from a disaster, it has been designed, instead, to be read in advance so that family members—particularly children—can be better prepared to survive a disaster and recover from its emotional after-shocks. The book makes sense. Every parent, guardian, and teacher should read it and institute its learning points. Preparation for disaster, after all, can prevent injuries, limit damage, and possibly save lives.

—Jeffrey T. Mitchell, Ph.D.
President, International Critical Incident Stress Foundation

Preface

Today, we cannot pick up a newspaper or watch television news without seeing or hearing about some type of disaster occurring somewhere in the world. Whether they are natural disasters, such as hurricanes, tornadoes, floods, fires, and earthquakes, or human-made disasters, such as terrorism, riots, rape, muggings, and so on, we and our loved ones will likely face disaster at some point in our lives. In the event of such occurrences, it is preparation that determines our survival—not only physical, but emotional as well.

In addition to those natural disasters that inevitably occur, acts of terrorism such as the bombings of the World Trade Center in New York City and the Federal Building in Oklahoma City are becoming all too common. During one four-year period, Los Angeles residents braved riots, floods, landslides, fires, and a major earthquake, not to mention the daily barrage of violent crime. Despite these incidents, however, the average Los Angelean is not prepared mentally, emotionally, or physically for the recurrence of these disasters. And they will happen again. Every resident of Los Angeles knows another earthquake will strike, just as people living in southern Florida know another strong hurricane is inevitable. Nonetheless, most go about their daily lives, unprepared for the next occurrence.

Only recently have large organizations such as the American Red Cross, the American Psychological Association, local departments of health and mental health, and several universities begun in earnest to study the mental and emotional effects that result from situations of extreme stress.

Through our work with individuals who have survived disaster, we, the authors, have learned that mental and emotional preparation is essential, especially for children. Those who prepare for disaster possess a readiness when it strikes—a readiness that enables them to survive and recover much more quickly than those who do not. Individuals who have not prepared and are hurt in a disaster experience a more positive emotional outcome if they receive help quickly. When help is not forthcoming, however, the outlook can be grim. Those who survive may seem fine to the observer, but they are often crippled emotionally, continually overwhelmed by events beyond their control.

Just knowing what to do in an emergency gives people a sense of control. Preparation is not expensive, painful, or time consuming. It can, however, be the difference between life and death. As parents, we devote our lives to helping our families, especially our children. Preparation for disaster may turn out to be one of the best ways we can protect them from future problems.

This book contains tips, systems, and methods for dealing with disaster. It outlines ways to prepare both physically and emotionally. To emphasize the grave importance of what is at stake in these situations, chapter 2 sets the stage by outlining how children react emotionally to disaster. From there, subsequent chapters explore specific disasters, and lay out specific ways for you, your children, and your whole family to heal.

1
Introduction

Life's experiences shape and mold everyone. Adults recall the highs and lows in their lives. They remember wonderful times with parents, or special gifts received. They remember being hurt—say, in a car accident—or being molested or robbed. They also remember traumatic events that scared them, such as their house catching on fire or any such life-threatening occurrence. Everyone's personalities today reflect the sum of their life experiences, both positive and negative. And when that experience is traumatic, it changes people permanently. Whether that change is minute or dramatic, when disaster strikes it leaves an indelible impression.

Hurricanes, fires, floods, earthquakes, riots, car bombings, rape, shootings—all natural and human-made disasters are traumatic, both for adults and for children. While some areas of the world see relatively few disasters, others are repeatedly bombarded. Witness the devastating hurricanes Florida residents endure, almost on a yearly basis. Southern California, in a short period of time, saw floods, fires, earthquakes, and riots. Oklahoma City and New York both witnessed the aftermath of car (truck) bomb explosions.

Terrorism is now a familiar word to most children. Every day, it seems, the news is filled with reports of people being hurt or killed by bombs, guns, cars, and poisonous gas, not to mention auto, plane, and train accidents. Because the frequency of such

1

disasters appears to be increasing, the need is more urgent than ever to teach parents how to protect and support children through disasters, and how to deal with the short- and long-term mental and emotional changes they elicit.

Although this book primarily addresses short-term effects of disaster, long-term effects can be equally devastating. Sometimes these effects are hidden. Human beings tend to want to forget or avoid unpleasant events or feelings and get on with their lives. Although this approach may seem logical, it simply doesn't work for individuals who were severely traumatized. Feelings of anxiety, depression, or posttraumatic stress can last for years. These feelings may be forgotten temporarily, but they emerge later, wanted or not.

Why Children Need Special Help

Adults react to disasters in a variety of ways. Some are able to decide under pressure what is best to do first—to help themselves, and then their children. Some, however, become disoriented, paralyzed, confused, or hysterical. What people bring to a situation, in terms of personality, experience in handling crises, and preparedness, determines how they react initially to a crisis, and how they handle the aftermath. This preparedness—mental and emotional—also conveys itself to children. Children quickly sense whether or not someone is in control. They pick up on a parent's hysteria, confusion, fear, and lack of preparation. While children and adults both suffer in a disaster, the effects on children can be more severe, because they do not yet possess the mental tools to understand what is happening. They depend on adults for guidance and control.

Children—especially young children—tend to be less verbal than adults. They may not have developed the vocabulary or conceptual understanding necessary to express what they are feeling. Because of this, adults can easily overlook, or even deny, their suffering. When a crisis occurs, most of the attention is usually given to the family member who demands it. Some children have said after a disaster that they didn't want to burden their parents with their feelings, and that their parents never asked. Parents must remember to ask how their children are feeling, during and after a crisis.

The terror and severe stress most children feel after a disaster manifest themselves in a number of ways, and in many different areas of their lives. Disturbed sleep habits, insomnia, nightmares, fear of sleeping alone, fear of the dark—all can be caused by severe stress. Actually, children's sleep is one of the most common areas to be affected. Parents also need to be aware of any significant change in behavior. Disasters affect children's play habits, and their relationships with friends, schoolmates, and other family members. Children can become irritable, act out aggressively, or withdraw. They may complain of physical ailments—ailments of unknown origin that even a physician cannot diagnose. And, like adults, children may develop long-term psychological disturbances. It is easy for parents, who are usually experiencing their own trauma and stress, to miss the symptoms of extreme stress in their children. It is important to remember that children are affected by the same types of stress parents are faced with in a disaster.

Why This Book Is for Parents

Children who have experienced a human-made or natural disaster exhibit the same symptoms as those who have been victimized by rape, incest, an accident, the loss of a loved one, or severe family dysfunction. Because most parents lack the tools to recognize and understand these symptoms, and to help their children heal, this book contains stories of others who have been through similar crises, and guidelines for parents on what to do and what to avoid.

Needs become fundamental in a disaster. Parents worry about the survival and injury of spouses and children first, and then return to a normal pattern of living as soon as possible. In a disaster, local, state, and sometimes federal agencies, as well as certain social agencies, usually assist those in need. The goal of these agencies is to help as many people as possible, as quickly as possible. For example, the Red Cross sets up shelters for those who are in need of shelter, food, medical assistance, and clothing.

Some families, however, may be temporarily left to fend for themselves. They may be unable to get to these shelters if, for example, they are without transportation or the roads are blocked. Or, if communications are down some people may not be able to find out where these shelters are located. Because of these and other difficulties after a disaster, and because the aid provided is sometimes short lived, parents are left to cope with the effects of a disaster themselves.

Unfortunately, most parents are neither trained nor prepared for the job. Few books, videotapes, or educational programs that explain what to do before, during, and after a disaster are designed specifically for parents; few offer instruction on how to protect children. The number of resources and programs to teach professionals how to intervene after a disaster is growing. Several books are now available for children to help explain what to expect after a disaster. Schools and local fire departments are increasingly offering programs to help children prepare physically for a disaster. But the amount of information available about mental and emotional preparation is still sorely lacking.

Because the outcome—in terms of physical and psychological survival—can vary widely, and because it is uniformly dependent upon preparation, this book is designed to help parents protect and support their children, and themselves, before, during, and after a disaster.

What Is a Disaster?

The use of the term disaster can, in some people's minds, range from a broken fingernail to a life-threatening event. In this book the term is defined as an event where there is great damage, loss, or death. It includes natural disasters, such as hurricanes, tornadoes, earthquakes, fires, and floods, as well as human-made disasters, such as riots, shootings, bombings, or other extreme acts of violence. It can include an accident that involves automobiles, planes, boats, trains, and so on. Whatever the ingredients, a disaster is intense and usually life threatening.

A disaster can affect an entire city or a single person. A personal disaster might involve a fatality or a near-death experience from an accident or injury. Some examples: escaping from a burning house, almost drowning, being held at gun point, surviving a car crash, or being attacked by an animal. A personal disaster does not usually include getting fired from a job, going through a divorce, being robbed while away from home, and so on. While this last group of occurrences may indeed be traumatizing, they would not necessarily be considered life threatening. Some may deem this definition inadequate. It seems most people are able to agree on the constitution of a major disaster that affects many people, but few are able to agree on a universal definition for a personal disaster. While the focus of this book is on large disasters, much of the information can be applied to coping with personal disaster, as well.

The Importance of Preparation

Preparation allows people to make decisions that can, at most, save lives and, at least, lessen injury or harm. Telling a child not to speak to strangers, for example, or not to get in a stranger's car may not only reduce the chance of that child being abused some day, it may save his or her life.

The question is often asked, Doesn't all this preparation make children anxious? While such a question is worth considering, the answer is unequivocally, No, if it is handled correctly. For years, children have been practicing fire drills at school. In certain parts of the country, they are also instructed in tornado or earthquake safety and preparation. With the rapid and pervasive communication available today—most specifically, television—most children are as aware of catastrophic events as their parents, and often as quickly. The purpose of advance training is as much to reduce anxiety as it is to save lives, by making sure each family member knows what to do in an emergency. It is part of the human condition: the more people know, the more they feel a small measure of control, and the less they worry or feel anxious.

Take, for example, a fire in a single-family home. If the children's bedrooms are on the second floor, teaching them to use emergency ladders may not only save their lives, it will likely reduce their fear about being trapped or being burned while running downstairs to reach the front door. By giving them an alternative for escape, they will feel more in control and, consequently, less afraid.

For those living in earthquake-prone areas, it is a good idea to keep a crowbar in the bedroom of every adult. If an earthquake strikes, family members can either break a window to get outside, or pry open a door that has jammed from the movement. If younger children are trapped, parents can use the crowbar to exit their own room and get to their children's rooms more quickly, which would reduce the amount of panic during such a frightening episode.

Sometimes the simplest tools can make a huge difference, both in terms of safety and self-confidence during a disaster. Safety lights, for example, that come on when the electricity goes off should be installed in every bedroom and hallway. They are inexpensive to purchase and operate, and can be essential when a disaster occurs in the middle of the night and the electricity has failed. Rather than fearing injury while feeling around in the dark, safety lights can illuminate furniture and broken glass, and can simplify and accelerate the process of rescuing children.

What Constitutes Trauma?

Trauma is an injury to the physical or psychological well-being of an individual. It means that someone has been hurt or upset to the degree that it severely affects the way they function, either mentally, emotionally, or physically, or a combination of the three. The stress created by trauma is often unexpected, sudden, and intense, and differs from other kinds of stress, which may be weaker and/or longer in duration.

People who have been through a disaster must contend not only with death, loss, and destruction, but also with the mental and emotional trauma that can persist long past the rebuilding of property. The initial trauma may subside, but often leaves in its place long-term posttraumatic stress or depression.

What Is Stress?

Stress is another of those words that has become popular in today's society. Since 1945, the time of Hans Selye, a physician who dedicated his career to the study of stress, society has adopted the term. People live it, suffer from it, and mention it at dinner parties. When chronic and severe, stress contributes to heart disease and failure; it is one of today's primary killers, particularly of men. Yet certain types of stress are essential to life. It is physical stress that holds the human body upright, for example. Interpersonal and family relationships can also generate stress. Stress is a type of demand on the body or the mind. Children experience stress at home and at school, by generating ideas, feelings, and actions. This type of stress, positive stress, differs in intensity from the type of stress experienced in a disaster, which is extreme stress, or traumatic stress.

Stress is the physical or emotional result of a reaction to something called the stressor, or that which causes the stress. It is this stressor which, when chronic or too severe, produces changes often seen in children and adults after a disaster. These changes may result in a temporary dysfunction, such as shock after nearly being hit by a car, or they may result in a permanent dysfunction if the reaction persists. For example, someone who survives a flood, fire, or earthquake may fear a recurrence so intensely that it causes him or her to move to an area with a smaller probability of such an event happening. If the stress causes a permanent, physical change, it is called psychosomatic, such as in the case of a psychosomatic disease—that is, an emotional disease that manifests itself physically. Such stress can also produce chronic emotional changes, such as mental diseases or disorders.

Where Does Stress Come from?

For some time, it has been known that environment and events affect people emotionally and physically. When financial, social, family, or personal pressures get too strong, people feel stress. The realization that lower stress levels can also cause physical harm is relatively recent, however. It seems society is finally beginning to accept what many already knew, that the mind and the body are interrelated and can seriously affect people if disturbed.

High-intensity stress can produce the same effect as low-intensity stress, but is sometimes more severe. A man who is almost hit by a car may react to the adrenaline suddenly being produced in his body, for example, experiencing such symptoms as a quickened heartbeat, perspiration, an urge to move quickly away from the scene, and so on. The human body's reaction to perceived danger is often the same as its reaction actual danger. The mind doesn't always differentiate between the two. People often feel afraid after the danger has passed.

What Are the Symptoms of Stress?

Although symptoms of stress will be discussed again later in this book, listed below are some of the symptoms of stress. Stress is exhibited in the exaggeration or abbreviation of almost any area of behavior.

Those Behaviors Might Be

1. Mental responses, such as being confused, disoriented, or unable to decide what to do next. This is a primary reason for preparation. When certain acts become automatic, such as the "duck and cover" exercise children learn in school, they can save lives. Consider Maria, a forty-two-year-old woman who was in a department store when an earthquake occurred. Surrounded by glass walls and a glass ceiling, she was terrified. She simply stood and screamed until the earthquake was over. Fortunately, she survived the falling glass. Had she not been confused and terrified, however, she might simply have crawled under the nearest table and gotten out of the way.

2. Emotional responses, such as being angry, fearful, depressed, and anxious. Feelings of stress strike quickly. They involve no thought, and they happen to everyone. What is important is to minimize the stress and continue

Reactions to Stress in Adults and Children		
SYMPTOMS	ADULTS	CHILDREN
Difficulty concentrating or focusing	Frequent	Frequent
Excessive crying	Occasional	Frequent
Overactive behavior	Occasional	Frequent
Isolation or keeping to oneself	Occasional	Frequent
Demands for affection	Occasional	Frequent
Complaints of illness or pain	Frequent	Frequent
Acting lethargic or apathetic	Frequent	Frequent
Regression to an earlier stage	Unusual	Frequent
Depression	Frequent	Occasional
Aggressive acting out behavior	Unusual	Frequent
Feelings of numbness	Occasional	Unusual
Upset stomach or diarrhea	Frequent	Frequent
Headaches	Frequent	Occasional
Fear or anxiety	Frequent	Frequent
Anger	Frequent	Unusual
Confusion and/or disorientation	Frequent	Occasional

to function. Take Gloria, a woman of thirty-four years, who was mildly hurt when a bookcase fell on her, but who was so frightened that she could not talk for several weeks. She sat around in a daze, staring at the walls around her. With support and warmth from others, she finally overcame her shock. It took extensive professional help to work through her feelings; some of those feelings, however, never left her. Gloria's life was forever changed; she limited where she went, and began to fear open spaces and crowds of people. Another example is Bill, a macho, twenty-eight-year-old who always felt in control of his life and was sure he could easily help his family if faced with disaster. But as the walls of his bedroom crumbled in an earthquake, he fell into an almost paralyzed state. The roar of the collapse, accompanied by complete darkness, left him disoriented and confused. The fact that he was totally out of control left him depressed. It took several years of professional help to regain his self-esteem and the self-confidence to live in a world that was not in his control.

3. Physical reactions, such as headaches, upset stomach, diarrhea, temporary blindness, numbness. These and other innumerable symptoms usually occur on a short-term basis and disappear with time.

4. Social reactions, such as withdrawing from social contact, or being irritable, aggressive, or acting out in some unusual way. These symptoms are common among children, and can last much longer than physical reactions. If persistent, professional help should be sought.

Most people exhibit some symptom or change in behavior as a result of stress. If the stress is too great, people will show many or all types of symptoms, most of which disrupt the pursuit of everyday life.

How Much Stress Is Too Much?

The difficulty of assessing stress is that what is stressful for one person may not be stressful for another; similarly, stress that is overwhelming for one person may be just right for another. Such is the case with occupations. Watching a painter or construction workers working atop a skyscraper, some may wonder how people can do such a thing for a living. But some people crave and enjoy high-stress occupations. Others enjoy staying home with three noisy children—an occupation many would consider overwhelming. The answer lies in the personality and makeup of the individual.

What is clear is that when people perceive a situation as too stressful they may have difficulty in normal, day-to-day functioning. For children who have not yet developed skills to deal with stress, preparing them to handle it may help them to avoid severe reactions later. These severe reactions are described in the American Psychiatric Association's DSM IV Manual as Acute Stress Disorder and Posttraumatic Stress Disorder.

What Is Acute Stress Disorder?

Both children and adults suffer from Acute Stress Disorder, which lasts from two days to four weeks. People who suffer from this disorder have been exposed to some upsetting incident in which they were threatened with serious injury or death, and felt intense fear, helplessness, or horror, as in a disaster. They might experience shock, a sense of being numb or detached. They might be in a daze and unable to recall the specific events of the disaster. They might have recurring flashbacks of the experience. They might try to avoid anything reminiscent of the disaster. They might have trouble concentrating, eating, or sleeping. They might be irritable and anxious. They might have difficulties socially, at work, or at school.

These are all common responses to disaster. In many cases, people's reaction to a disaster is more important than the physical result of the disaster, as long as they are not physically hurt. During that two-day to four-week period most people are able to regroup, pull themselves together, and return to their daily routine and help their children to do the same. But not everyone will recover so quickly.

What Is Posttraumatic Stress Disorder?

Some people simply cannot get over the tragedy they were involved in. No amount of comforting and support seem to work. These are the individuals who suffer from Posttraumatic Stress Disorder and need professional help. When a person has moved beyond Acute Stress Disorder, when the effects of a stressful situation last longer than one month, it is considered posttraumatic stress. If the symptoms last between one and three months it is acute posttraumatic stress. If they last more than three months it is chronic.

Again, the individual may have experienced some event that involved actual or the threat of death or serious injury, and has responded with intense fear, helplessness, or horror. In children, such an event may cause agitation or disorderly behavior. The person may have recurring memories and may avoid anything associated with the event. Most important, the event has caused the individual to be disturbed and upset at work, in social situations, at school, or in other areas.

By preparing themselves and their children in advance, parents can greatly reduce the severity of these symptoms by being aware of what to expect in their own and their children's reactions. Everyone hopes that disaster will never affect them directly, but events on the daily news suggests otherwise. Parents may be able to avoid permanent damage to their families in the future by making adequate preparations.

Why Do Some People Handle Disasters Better Than Others?

That different individuals handle disasters differently is well known. One spouse may deal with crises quite differently than the other; one may remain relatively calm while the other becomes upset and unable to function. Children also handle disasters differently, because of differences in age, personality, and understanding. The important question to answer is, How is it that some people recover quickly, while others seem permanently disabled by a disaster? Until a person has lived through a disaster, there may be no way of knowing how he or she will react. But a number of factors enable accurate predictions. And those predictions can help parents to prepare for the actual event. If, for example, a mother knows that her eldest son will likely panic, she would be wise not to assign him a vital duty during a crisis, and to be ready to comfort and support him when the crisis happens. Knowing in advance how people may react can be instrumental in saving their lives. In a family of four or more, the question may be who to get to first when a disaster happens.

Personality

Personality plays an important role in predicting who will respond appropriately during and after a disaster. In general, people who perceive themselves as being in charge of their own happiness and security respond better than those who perceive others as having control. In other words, people with independent personalities do better than those with dependent personalities. However, those with independent personalities can't be so independent as to deny their own vulnerability, weaknesses, or need for help. Independence does not mean feeling invincible. In fact, people who act as though they feel invincible may be disguising their true feelings of insecurity and dependency.

Sensitivity

Sensitivity is another factor that can influence the intensity of people's reactions and speed of recovery. People who are sensitive or hypersensitive are in a constant state of alertness. They move to alarm or intense states of fear at the slightest provocation. Children or adults who are fearful of loud noises, the dark, unfamiliar surroundings, new people, or other changes in their own environment may be particularly affected by a disaster.

Some individuals crave excitement. They seem to love situations that require extraordinary effort and quick response. These lovers of high stress do well when faced with disaster, because it requires them both to take charge and to act immediately. In contrast, low-stress people may become confused, disorganized, or disoriented in a disaster, partly because quick thinking and action is required. These people may not like to take charge and may be more comfortable taking a dependent role in a disaster. Volunteers for organizations such as the Red Cross and fire departments typify high-stress people. These are not disaster junkies; rather they are altruistic people who love dealing with excitement. They deal well with stress and enjoy bringing order out of chaos.

In most families, one parent has learned to take charge or to be the responsible person when decisions have to be made. These are not just people who don't mind responsibility, but are people who actually seek it out. They enjoy being in charge and making decisions.

Children, the elderly, and handicapped people are often at risk both during and after disasters, because they are dependent upon others for their support and safety. At the start of their lives, children depend on their parents for emotional and physical survival; only gradually do they gain physical and emotional independence. By the same token, elderly people with failing eyesight, hearing, and mobility can easily become frightened during a disaster and may suffer long-term negative effects. The same can happen to those who are handicapped. Despite their ever-increasing independence, the handicapped have a forced dependency in a disaster, particularly when the failure of electricity and other conveniences make their mobility impossible.

Age

The younger a child, the more dependent and sensitive he or she usually is. There are some exceptions, however. Some children under the age of four may not feel threatened by the actual happening, but rather, may react to their parents' anxiety. Because young children do not, as yet, have a sense of the permanency of death, their reactions may not be as severe as, say, a child between the ages of five and ten who is fully aware of the concept and permanency of death, and is still dependent emotionally upon adults. Also, younger children may be less able to verbalize their fears, frustrations, or losses.

Perhaps one of the most critical times for children comes as they enter preadolescence. Between the ages of nine and twelve, children begin to assert their independence by being mouthy, argumentative, defiant, and rebellious. Although not all preadolescents exhibit the same negative behaviors, most show some variation on the theme. These children have already developed the verbal and cognitive skills to comprehend what is happening. They are beginning to move away from their parents, but are neither fully dependent upon adults nor able to stand on their own. Their situation is extremely vulnerable, in part, because society does little to clarify whether they are adults or children, and what is expected of them. Trauma at this time can set them back months or years, or alter their personality permanently.

Parents differ on how they see their children and what they demand from them. Adolescence is a time when parents show anger toward their children when they do not live up to expectations. When disaster strikes, preadolescents have been known either to regress to an earlier age, or, surprising to parents, act in a more responsible manner and help take charge of the situation. This can also be a variation in personality.

Experience and Training

Experience can be either helpful or a hindrance. If a child has survived an intense experience such as a hurricane, earthquake, fire, or flood, and has suffered no ill effects, he or she will be more familiar with what to expect and better able to function effectively during the next disaster. If a child has experienced a variety of traumas, such as escaping a house fire, surviving an auto accident, being lost for a period of time, or healed from a broken bone, and has recovered nicely, he or she may be better equipped to handle a larger disaster. If, on the other hand, a child has had a slow or poor recovery, he or she may be at risk during a larger disaster. The child who has had poor reactions to smaller crises may need more preparation and training than a child who has had a more positive reaction.

Through experience, an individual can gradually learn to stay calm, think clearly, and act appropriately under pressure and high stress. Remembering past exercises or techniques before a big test, championship game, speech, stage performance, or an emergency—these are some safe ways to practice lowering anxiety, remaining calm, achieving clarity, and acting effectively.

Education

Education is immensely helpful for both children and adults. The combination of information and practice may be the most effective method for surviving a disaster and minimizing posttraumatic stress. Human beings are created to learn. Giving them information about what a particular disaster looks, sounds, smells, and feels like activates the basic learning mechanisms inherent in the human body. Coupled with information about what to do before, during, and after a disaster, this kind of training is highly effective. Suggested readings for this type of education are listed at the end of this book.

Preparation

Preparation is key. Preparation includes practice and training, as well as education. All the evidence clearly shows that those who are prepared mentally, emotionally, physically, and materially, fare better than those who are not. Race car drivers usually drive better than amateur drivers, because they are educated about the dynamics of driving, practice under high-stress situations, review their performances, and adjust their preparation based on that performance. Over time, this sequence—preparation, experience, review, adjustment—lowers the risk of potential disaster and teaches people what to do when a disaster occurs.

Psychological Health

Psychological health also plays an important role. A child or an adult who is depressed, fearful, or lonely will be at greater risk for trauma during and after a disaster. Traditionally, children who feel unloved, rejected, alone, or abandoned, as well as children from insecure, unstable, or violent homes do not fare well in a disaster. On the other hand, children who feel good about themselves, children from stable and supportive families, do. Where there is good communication, love, comfort, closeness, and trust, security and growth abound. When children are shown respect, they learn to respect themselves and are able to act in a more independent manner.

Parents should always be concerned with the emotional health of their children. Rather than assume that children will change as they grow, parents must nurture the emotional health and independence of their children. Ask yourself, What would my children do today if a disaster occurred? If the answer is not to your liking, it is time to start teaching them to think independently and to prepare to make decisions when you are not available to help them. It will be time well spent. It could save their lives as well as yours.

2

Children's Emotional Reaction to Crisis

What Might Your Children Feel and How Would They Show It?

While a disaster will strongly influence any child's life, as with any adult, a child's reaction to any given situation depends on what he or she brings to that situation, and on how prepared he or she is.

It is difficult to evaluate children in a disaster situation without prior information about their behavior before the disaster. It is parents who are usually in the best position to get this information. For example, children who repeatedly attempt suicide often have a history of severe difficulties. Children who come from homes that are loving, nonabusive, and nonthreatening handle disasters better than children who are continually stressed, abused, depressed, or anxious. When children are traumatized—that is, threatened and unable to cope or defend themselves—

17

they are less able to handle disaster. If childhood traumas go unrecognized and untreated, later behavior reflects these inner conflicts. Although these traumas originated from the outside, from the child's environment, and may have occurred quickly, some children may take a long time, possibly years, to recover. Secure and happy children have a better chance of dealing with a disaster, handling themselves well, and recovering quickly.

The primary concern of most people, including children, is their own personal safety. Parents must reassure children that they will be protected. Even if the effects of the disaster continue, parents must reassure children that they will be safe.

Regression

While most people can show signs of some type of regression, it is most common in children. After the Los Angeles earthquake of 1994, many parents reported their nineteen-year-old son or daughter sleeping in their bed or bedroom. Other examples: young children who have given up thumb sucking may start again, or children may resume bed wetting. Clinging and immature behavior is common. Nightmares and disturbed sleep are common. What stands out is the regression—that is, the child used to engage in a certain behavior, grew out of it, and is now starting to exhibit the same behavior again.

Quietness and Lack of Emotional Expression

One of the errors parents can make after a disaster is to deal primarily with family members who make the most noise or are the most demanding. Some children handle stress by becoming quiet and withdrawn. They may have feelings of fear or terror, but outwardly show nothing. Parents tend to ignore these children, believing their silence means that everything is fine, but these are the children who are likely in the most need of assistance. Sometimes they just need to be held or comforted. Sometimes they need to talk and express how they feel. Beware the quiet child, especially if everyone around him or her is upset or afraid.

Lethargy and Apathy

Another common response among children is a change in behavior from energetic and active, to slow, lethargic, and apathetic. The best way to know if there is a problem is to notice the changes. Is the child acting differently now than before the disaster occurred? If the child looks different and acts differently, there is likely a problem that needs to be dealt with. It may take a great deal of time to get the child to express his or her feelings, so it may be possible to delegate this job to an older child or another parent. Whichever the case, early intervention can be very helpful in preventing further problems.

Complaints of Illness or Pain

Whenever a child complains of illness or pain, parents need to pay attention, particularly after a disaster. It may be an attention-getting maneuver, but it may also represent some damage not immediately visible to parents. Think of it as the child sending a message. It may be complex, and difficult to decode, but pay attention to it. If nothing is found during a physical examination, continue to listen; the child may be crying for emotional help.

Increased Demands for Attention

One change in behavior that parents immediately detect is an increase in the demand for attention. When afraid, children cling and become dependent. They may not want to be alone, wanting to sleep with or be in the same room with the parent. This type of behavior can be annoying and tiresome, especially if constant, but the child is expressing his or her need for reassurance and support, in the only way he or she knows how.

Isolation

Sometimes, the reverse becomes evident. Children who were sociable before a disaster may isolate themselves from friends, family, and the world, staying in their bedrooms listening to music or watching television. This type of behavior is an attempt at putting the world in order. It is as though other people offer too much stimulation. These children, unable to handle this stimulation, need to be alone.

Displays of Fear and Anxiety

Although a disaster may affect all members of a family, their reactions may differ dramatically. Some children withdraw. Some cry. Some deny that anything bad really happened and some show a tremendous fear and anxiety. These are the children who most need reassurance and comforting, but who also may reject it. There are ways to deal with these problems, which are discussed later in this book. There is a wide range of fears that children display, from fear of disaster to fear of the future. Their worry is that the disaster might happen again, and that it might be worse the next time.

Overactive or Silly Behavior

People become restless when they are under stress. Children are no different, except that their control over impulses is less developed. Children, especially boys, tend to show stress by becoming overactive and sometimes silly to gain attention and to release tension. If this behavior is different than their behavior prior to the disaster, pay attention to it.

Excessive Crying

Crying is the most common response of distressed, hurt, or scared children. Crying is a healthy way for children to communicate that something is bothering them. What parents should do is not stop their children from crying—that is, not forbid crying—but comfort and hold them until they feel safe and secure. The crying will usually stop, especially if there is no threat of the disaster reoccurring.

Difficulty in Concentration and Focus

Just as adults have difficulty concentrating and focusing at work after a disaster has struck, children have the same difficulty at school. This is a normal reaction, but one that becomes disruptive if the child does not recover quickly. The best way to help such a child is to use any means possible to allow him or her to express feelings—methods such as talking, drawing, and playing.

How Do Children Show Symptoms of Stress After a Disaster?

Although the term *children* may mean any age from birth to eighteen years old, reactions to disasters vary with age. Below are customary reactions among children, according to specific age groups.

Children Ages One to Five

Each age group has basic tasks to accomplish, and specific basic concerns. This is the group that is most responsive to their parents' behavior. For children of this age, the primary fears are abandonment, loss of a parent, and physical pain. If a parent becomes very upset or out of control during a disaster the effects on a young child can be overwhelming. The younger the child, the more he or she is affected by changes in the parents, or adults, in his or her world. Children of this age group do not intellectually understand what is happening. What they do understand are moods and feelings, the fears and anxieties, of the adults around them. These are the children most vulnerable in disasters.

These children may show
fear and anxiety
an inability to express in words their feelings and needs
loss of appetite
regression to old habits, such as thumb-sucking
loss of control of bladder or bowels, or constipation
increased clinging and attention-getting behaviors, increased
   dependence on parents
new fears of darkness, animals, people, or places
fear of being alone

Parents can help these children by
becoming aware of their change in behavior
touching and holding them, to increase feelings of security
   and comfort
listening and talking to them

playing with them

giving them additional attention

letting them talk about what happened, again and again and
again

allowing them to express feelings through talking, drawing,
and playing

helping them get back into a comfortable, familiar routine

allowing special privileges for a limited period of time, such
as sleeping in the same room or bed with parents

Children Ages Five to Eleven

Children this age also fall back or regress to earlier behaviors.

They may show
babyish behavior
dependency on parents
whining
irritability
demanding and attention-getting behavior
nightmares
avoidance of friends
aggressive behavior with friends at school or in the neighborhood
fighting with siblings to get parental attention
inability to focus and concentrate at school
anger, especially at parents
anxiety, which can manifest itself in many forms

Because children of this age group are much more verbal, they
will often make their needs known to parents. They may be able
to answer questions or ask for what they need. Parents can help a
great deal by listening carefully and noting changes in behavior.

Parents can help these children by
listening and talking to them, and answering their questions.
playing games with them
touching and holding them, if they allow it
being less demanding about chores, school, or the usual routines, for a brief period of time

resuming the usual routines at home when appropriate
explaining the source of their own irritation, if applicable
discussing family plans for the near future

Children Ages Eleven and Above

It becomes more difficult to specify the behavior of children beyond age eleven. Some are immature and react like younger children. Others react in a more mature fashion, like young adults. Still others mimic the behavior of the parent of the same sex. There is often a ripple effect throughout the family, as though feelings were contagious. As these children learn to deal with their feelings, the fear and discomfort they feel subside and recovery progresses.

Older children may experience
difficulty sleeping
depression
denial of feelings, such as, "It doesn't bother me."
loss of the feeling of security
feelings of guilt that others were hurt more than they were
feelings of anger and irritability without knowing who to be
    angry at
feelings of numbness, or not allowing themselves to feel any-
    thing
fear of a reoccurrence
flashbacks, or the tendency to relive the incident
increased fighting among siblings or with friends
other unusual changes in feelings or behavior

Trying to help children eleven or older can be difficult. For most children of this age group, talking and listening are the most effective techniques. Where there has been the loss of a loved one or severe trauma, they will need months and sometimes years to recover. Explain that whatever they feel at the moment will get better with time.

Parents can help these children by explaining that intense feelings are like waves; they are big and close together in the beginning, but get smaller and farther apart as time goes on. Tell them that unpleasant thoughts and feelings come at all different times of the day and night, and warn them about sudden mood swings. Encourage them to allow and acknowledge their feelings, whenever they can, wherever they are, and as much as they are able. Tell them that by letting their waves of feelings wash over them, rather than resisting them, the moods will pass faster. Explain that if they resist, or suppress, feelings too quickly, they risk transferring them to other areas of their life. Tell them that if they are at work or school, or in a place where they do not feel comfortable expressing their feelings, they should simply identify what they are remembering or feeling and let themselves remember and feel it at the first available opportunity.

Most people, and especially teenagers, associate crying and being fearful with being weak or immature. Reassure teenagers that crying is the human body's natural and healthy way of processing intense feelings. Tears are only signs of an overflowing heart.

Parents can help these children by
spending additional time with them
touching and holding them, if they will allow it
being less demanding about chores, school or the usual routines, for a brief period
resuming the usual routines at home as appropriate

3

What to Do before a Disaster

Preparing Mentally for Disaster

It only takes a moment of terror to change brain chemistry. Preparation can reduce the feelings of terror enormously. How do we prepare ourselves mentally?

Discussion

Parents should discuss various types of incidents, large and small, that they or their children may face. Most have never gone through the exercise of thinking about how they'd react if they were mugged, or raped, or if their house caught fire. Would they play the role of victim? Would they repair the damage themselves and contact the proper authorities? Thinking in advance of the unthinkable is a worthwhile exercise in minimizing the damage to both parents and their children.

Parents frequently ask, Doesn't this traumatize the child? The answer is, No, if the exercise is presented as a precaution. Children are already made aware of most of these situations by television coverage. Be prepared—it's not only the Boy Scout motto, but also a vital strategy for protection. Discuss the possibility of a disaster, both small and large, with children. The very act of thinking about it, which is essentially a rehearsal of the moment, may prove helpful later on.

Rehearsal

The next step after mental preparation is rehearsing an event before it happens. Rehearsal includes devising a plan to ensure that a spouse and/or children are safe, and that they know what to do. Being mentally prepared is only the first. Physical rehearsal ensures a family's ability to function during and after a disaster. Although surprises will always play a part, rehearsal reduces the number of unexpected events.

What to Do When the Unexpected Happens

No matter how much people prepare, they will always face unexpected events. They can expect and prepare for a hurricane, for example, but still be overwhelmed by its intensity or destructiveness. Similarly, escape and safety measures can be well planned and rehearsed, but when the disaster strikes, people can find that everything has changed. During the 1994 earthquake in Los Angeles, for instance, many knew what to do, but were unable to do it. The surprise of waking up at 4:31 a.m. to a terrible noise and a shaking house meant that not everyone would be able to get outside, or even to a doorway, for safety. Part of mental preparation is taking into account that the correct thing is not always possible, and being prepared to make immediate adjustments for the unexpected.

What to Expect in Terms of Sights, Sounds, Smells, and Others' Reactions

Most can depend on getting the necessary information about what to expect in fires, floods, earthquakes, tornadoes, and so on. What is often lacking is specific information—the intensity of sights, sounds, smells, or possible reactions to others' hysteria. Knowing what fire is, is quite different than knowing what to expect from a fire, the actual feeling of heat, the immense devastation, the stinging eyes, or the difficulty in breathing. One woman lost her house to a fire, but was more upset by her cat being burned. No one can prepare for every circumstance, but it is helpful to know what to expect, even in the form of a description.

How Pressure Affects Thinking and Memory

As people prepare mentally for disaster, they must also prepare for the internal changes that occur. A natural consequence of going through any traumatic incident is change. This change manifests itself in what is called impaired cognitive functioning. Stable, sensible people suddenly find they can no longer think or communicate in a sensible way under pressure. They may or may not be feeling physical pain. Sometimes it is simply viewing mass destruction or personal disaster that hinders thought and communication. It only takes a moment to lose control; it may take months or years of memories, nightmares, or reliving the moment to heal or recover from the bad feelings created by that loss.

Exercises

1. Based on the climate, determine what disasters are common to your area—for example, fires, floods, hurricanes, tornadoes, earthquakes, thunderstorms, or extreme heat or cold. Add these to the list of more personal disasters such as house fires, auto accidents, and being victimized by violent crimes.

2. Make a detailed plan about what every member of the family should do. If your plans involve friends or extended family members, be sure they are aware of them and will cooperate fully.

3. For the first four weeks, sit down as a family once a week and review your plans for any specific disaster. You might offer rewards for the those that can memorize the plans first (making it into a game may get younger children more involved). For resistant teenagers, remind them that their resistance could endanger the lives of the rest of the family, or simply let them know that their social life on weekends may depend on their cooperation.

4. Once everyone is familiar with the plan, schedule these meetings once a month. Twelve reviews a year is not overkill, and will help keep everyone's memory sharp. Remember, people forget under pressure. Frequent and realistic practice is essential for

effective performance. By the time you are practicing once a month, rehearsals can be completed in fifteen minutes or less.

5. When you review, make sure each child, independently, can explain what he or she is supposed to do. You might have everybody sit with their eyes closed and imagine what is in the disaster kit, or where the food is, the water is, and so on.

6. Every six months or so, practice lighting a flare, bandaging a wound, using a fire extinguisher, or shutting off the power, water, or gas (if you know how to reignite all the pilot lights). You may also want to recycle your food and water supplies.

An Example

Henry Northcutt, his wife, Julie, and their three children live in an area of Texas that has seen floods, drought, and hurricanes during the twenty-five years he's lived there. In the last flood he lost his house, his barn, and a good portion of his livestock. He took all this in stride, but when it came time to evacuate, and they couldn't find their six-year-old daughter, Theresa, Henry panicked. He decided to stay with a neighboring rancher and look for her while he sent his wife and their two boys to a shelter on higher ground.

It was almost nightfall when, through the pouring rain, Henry heard his daughter's cry for help. Theresa had gone to retrieve a young calf that was stuck in a muddy field some distance from their house. In the process, she had gotten herself stuck and was now very frightened. Henry and his neighbor were able to gather enough rocks, sticks, and tree branches to fashion a crude bridge and eventually free her. Knowing that time was short, they hurried back to the house. There had been a flood warning earlier in the day and the fire department had been by to tell everyone to evacuate before nightfall.

By the time they arrived at the house, Henry could see that the barn was already flooding and the power was out. His mind shifted back to the flood ten years ago, which pretty much ruined the first floor of his two-story house. He focused on the escape at hand. He knew the road would be washed out, much too deep for his sedan-style car to get through. He figured he could wait it out until morning when people would be by to rescue them in boats. What he didn't know, however, was that the levy one mile north of his house would partially fail and eventually the flood would end up killing fifteen people in his community and destroying a great deal of property.

About an hour after Henry, his neighbor, and Theresa arrived at the house, the water began to pour in. They hurriedly moved things upstairs and established a lookout on the balcony off the master bedroom, planning to ride things out. Henry heard it only a few seconds before he felt it, the sound of powerful, rushing water as it crashed against the house with a terrible noise. The house shook violently, leaning under immense strain as the water smashed through the downstairs windows and encircled the house. But it remained standing. The terror they felt at that moment was like nothing any of them had ever experienced. For an instant they were absolutely still. Henry thought they were all about to die.

It took only a few seconds, but everything seemed to move in slow motion. Henry grabbed his daughter as he yelled to the neighbor, "To the roof!" He ran to the balcony, leaped the railing and jumped to the roof. His movements were almost catlike. The neighbor followed, clutching the flashlight he was carrying. For the next nine hours, the three of them would sit on the roof praying that God would spare their lives.

They knew the authorities were aware that they had not made it to the shelter and that Julie would be trying to get help for them. They also knew it was raining too hard for a rescue team to find them, there, atop the roof, in the dark. Alone, wet, and cold they huddled together, watching and listening for any sight or sound of the rescue team. They also watched what was now the mightiest of rivers swell around them. They prayed that their house would remain intact.

At approximately three o'clock, the rain began to diminish, turning slowly to a drizzle. This gave them some hope; the water had reached the edge of the roof. Shortly before five, they spotted the light in the distance that turned out to be the helicopter. With the flashlight, they were able to signal the rescue team; within minutes they were lifted into the helicopter and flown to safety.

It took nearly two weeks before the Northcutts could return home. Tractors were brought in to help clear the mud and debris. The damage was assessed; insurance companies were contacted.

Representatives from state, local, and federal agencies were on the scene. Just about everything within several miles was destroyed. Many families put their property up for sale and moved out of the area. But Henry and his family decided to stay.

Over the course of the next year, Henry rebuilt his house and barn. Slowly, the family began to put their lives back together. Henry made a few additions to his property. He constructed a steel pole that ran the height of his house near the side where the upstairs balcony was. Attached to the pole was a twelve-foot aluminum boat with a strong outboard motor. It was attached in a way that would allow the boat to rise along the pole if flooding occurred. In the boat he kept rain gear, signaling devices, two oars, rope, life jackets, extra fuel, and a variety of other supplies. A skylight was built in each of the upstairs rooms, and a portable ladder is kept under the bed or in the closet, so that anyone would have access to the roof in an emergency. On the roof itself Henry had built a small watertight box that contains a six-person inflatable raft and much of the same equipment that is in the boat.

In addition, Henry decided to add to his basement a special room that is completely enclosed in steel-reinforced concrete with a steel door and a venting system. He built this because tornadoes come through the area periodically. His property had never been hit by one, but he is not taking any chances.

Every three months, Henry and his entire family rehearse climbing to the roof and inflating the raft. They inspect the flashlights; test the signaling devices, examine and try on the rain gear, and start the motor on the boat. Henry hopes he will never have to use his equipment, but he is aware of the dangers that exist in his area, and he is now prepared.

Preparing Emotionally for Disaster

Self-Examination Before a Disaster

An excellent way of preparing for disaster is to evaluate certain aspects of yourself before something happens. How do you handle everyday ups and downs? Do you get upset easily? Are you able to think clearly when something awful happens? For most, the answers are, Not very well, Yes, and Not really. Most people are not at their best in an accident or disaster. When an event is expected, however, and there is enough time to think about it, those same people do a much better job of dealing with crisis. That is precisely the message of this book. Take a moment to think. What would you do if your child was hit by a car, or if you walked into your kitchen because you smelled smoke and found the whole kitchen ablaze? What you do in the next minute or two may save your house, or even your child's life. Programming yourself in advance so you know how to react and how to deal with your feelings can help you take the appropriate action. For example, calling 911 rather than moving a child with a spinal injury could save his or her life. And calling 911 for the fire department, instead of trying to extinguish an oil fire with water, could save your house.

How Are You Going to Feel When Disaster Strikes?

By their very nature, disasters create fear and sometimes unusual, unexpected reactions. It is natural to try to save children from being hurt, but parents can do little if they are paralyzed with fear. Thinking through reactions in advance is helpful because it provides both a sense of control and some programmed action to take. Fear can be controlled temporarily by having a plan. Planning puts an order to thought, it prioritizes actions during chaos. It reestablishes control.

Feeling afraid or overwhelmed is a natural reaction to a disaster. But having steps to follow diminishes that fear and clears the way to solving a problem constructively. For example, if there is a fire in your kitchen, can you tell whether it is controllable? If the fire is limited to a small area, it can be put out with a fire extinguisher. If it is not, calling 911 for professional help is the best alternative. Emotionally, people can handle a situation better when they have a plan for resolving the problem.

Reactions to Disaster

One of the strangest results of disasters is that people are often ashamed of their reactions. They feel they should have been smarter, or braver. They feel they shouldn't have cried or become hysterical. In essence, they are judgmental about their own emotional reactions.

The fact is, few people are able to think clearly and logically about what to do in a totally unexpected situation. It is normal to feel severe anxiety, fear, or even doom. No one is ever totally prepared for their own reactions, especially if they are hurt in a disaster. Even in the presence of adequate warning, until one has experienced a hurricane, for example, the massive destruction it can cause is incomprehensible.

Average people react differently to threat, real and perceived. They may deny that it could really happen. They may become overwhelmed and hysterical, or terribly, silently afraid. The range of response is wide, but those who have a plan in advance fare better than those who never think about their reactions. What is important to realize is that by gaining control of their own feelings, people are better able to help those they love most.

Common Fears

Most people in this country live their lives in an ordered society. They each have certain roles to play. They get up every morning and go to work, either at an office or at home. They come home in the evening for dinner, enjoy their families, watch television, or otherwise try to enjoy their lives. When a disaster—large or small—strikes, it immediately upsets that order. Disaster is usually unexpected. Emotionally, people's immediate task is to save themselves and put their lives back in order. This becomes difficult when the disaster is ongoing. People fear being hurt, abandoned, or—what may be most disturbing—the unknown. In an earthquake, a roof could fall in. In a hurricane or tornado, a roof could be blown off. Not knowing what will happen is so frightening because the order of most people's lives creates the illusion that future events are known or can be predicted. Parents have the added fear of not being able to get to their frightened children in a disaster. They may not know for sure what is happening to them.

Although fear is a normal reaction in these situations, it becomes problematic when it leads to hysteria, loss of control, or temporary paralysis. People's fear of injury or of injury to their children is very powerful; nobody should be blamed for their reactions. Everyone should, however, learn to prepare themselves. Thinking ahead about what to do and even writing down those steps can help even the most fearful through those initial terrifying moments, until control can be regained.

How People Differ in Their Emotional Reactions to Disaster

Both parents and children show a wide range of normal reactions in a disaster. One parent may be frightened initially, but almost immediately takes control of his or her own feelings and begins to do whatever is necessary to preserve both the family's life and property. These individuals are the ones that have prepared themselves for almost any eventuality. They have flashlights and know ways to safely exit their homes. They do not live with the fear of disaster, but, knowing the kinds of events that occur in their community, are prepared for whatever happens. Another type of parent becomes initially paralyzed and is not able to do anything at all. With some time, this type of parent will eventually return to normal and can then be helpful.

Then there is the parent who becomes hysterical and rushes through the house to protect the children, but does nothing constructive because he or she is so upset. This type of parent may simply scream and scream until he or she gains some measure of control. This type of behavior is not only not helpful, but can be harmful by making others in the family anxious.

In general, those in crisis feel a natural reaction of intense fear of impending death or injury—their own, or their family's. What not all parents are able to do is use their knowledge and skill to help themselves or their family until they are over their initial panic. To be terrified in a disaster is normal. But preparation can minimize the damage that may occur.

Emotional Preparation

Rehearsal under conditions as authentic as possible is the best preparation. Police, fire, military, and emergency personnel are trained extensively under emergency situations to strengthen their mental and emotional responses during stressful events. Most people never have the opportunity to receive such formal training, but there are some things that can be done.

Exercises

1. If you have an opportunity to visit an amusement park where there are roller coasters or exciting rides, you can use these for partial training. Some theme rides have special effects that mimic disaster—things falling, exploding, and catching on fire, all with loud noises. Most of the time, the effects are realistic and dramatic enough to involve you in the moment. If you want to train yourself mentally and emotionally, go through the ride refocusing your attention on potential areas of safety and escape, and suppressing any fear or tension. See if you can do the whole ride in a focused and relaxed state of mind. This will likely take practice. Simply repeating the ride a number of times will diminish the excitement because the events will be predictable. This predictability has a calming or soothing effect, and provides a sense of control.

If the ride is suitable for your children and they are willing to go on it, ask them to see if they can identify two or three areas of safety, as though it were a real disaster. This could take two or three times on the ride. Make a game out of it and offer a special prize for the child who can give three good answers. If one or more of the children resist, don't insist.

2. Recall from your memory any emergencies or disasters that you have experienced. Go back in your mind and relive the experience, but this time change any action you took that you think would have improved the situation. Go through the events not with fear, but with a focused attention on what needed to be done. Eliminate tears, crying, screaming, or any panicky behavior. All the emotions can be released after the event is over and everyone is safe.

3. Recall any pressure-filled moments in sports, school, or at your job when you had to perform. It may have been a championship game, a speech or performance in front of a large crowd, or some project that needed to be completed by a certain deadline. Recall the emotions associated with that event. See if you can stir them up again, only this time go through the events in

your head with clarity and focus, and without fear. Stand up and go through the motions physically as you recall the events. This can be a type of rehearsal and, if repeated enough, will help you prepare.

4. If you have an opportunity to put yourself in pressure-filled situations that don't endanger your life, or the lives of others, such as sports, public presentations, or simply trying something new, practice focusing under pressure and controlling your emotions. Taking classes in acting, public speaking, martial arts, dance, and so on, will require you to perform in front of others.

5. If you have any particular phobias, you might consider working specifically on them, perhaps with some professional help. Fear of elevators, flying, small spaces, wide open spaces, the dark, snakes (practice with nonpoisonous snakes!)—all provide a readily available source to practice managing anxiety. Learning how to overcome phobias would greatly strengthen your abilities, and possibly those of your child, to handle a disaster.

6. If you have an opportunity to visit the site of a previous disaster, spend a little time imagining what it must have been like for those involved. Look around and imagine that you were caught in various places at the site, and what you would do to protect yourself or your child. See if you can discern which areas were safe. (Be sure to not go to a site too soon. You must not interfere with emergency personnel or equipment, or trespass on private property or protected areas.)

7. Occasionally, hospitals have disaster drills to prepare for large numbers of victims coming into a hospital at one time. They use volunteers, putting them in splints, casts, and bandages, and carrying them on stretchers. It is all make-believe; the "victims" are usually volunteers and family members of the hospital staff. This is an excellent way for you and your family to prepare, as children are often part of these rehearsals. You can call any local hospital near you to see if they have a schedule for these events.

An Example

Joanne Rodriguez, a single mother of two, lived through the January 1994 earthquake in California. She lived on the second floor of a three-story apartment building. When the earthquake hit, the building collapsed, partially crushing the underground parking and the first floor. The second floor was on the ground and some portions of the third floor were left leaning against the neighboring apartment building.

The quake hit in the early morning hours before daylight. It lasted at least thirty seconds or more. Everything went dark before the shaking finished; almost immediately the building collapsed. Joanne recalls jumping out of bed but then almost simultaneously being thrown back by the falling building. Everything was tossed to one end of the room, herself included. She was hit by a small television and a drawer from her dresser. She could hear one of her daughters screaming as she called out to them. Her older daughter had been knocked unconscious.

Joanne crawled past fallen furniture into her daughters' room, adjacent to hers. She cut herself a couple of times on broken glass and other objects, but kept moving, slowly, all the while reassuring one of her daughters to stay calm. It took several minutes to reach their room. When she arrived, she could tell that everything had been thrown upside down. Maria, the younger daughter, was clinging to a bedpost that had been turned on its side. When she saw her mother, Maria crawled to her, desperately reaching out to touch her mom. Joanne held her tightly, but realized that she couldn't see Rosa, her older daughter. She began calling out to her.

After a little exploring, she found Rosa beneath a mattress that had fallen on top of her when she was thrown from her bed. She was unconscious, but breathing. Joanne took a blanket that was nearby and wrapped Rosa in it. She could see through the bedroom windows that a block wall prevented them from going through. So, through a combination of walking and crawling Joanne and Maria were able to make it to the hallway; Joanne carried Rosa. Fortunately, they were able to open the front door. The hallway was in better shape and they were able to move more quickly. At this point Rosa woke up, but was unaware of what was happening.

A few other people were in the hallway; echoes of screams and crying filled the corridor. One man had a flashlight and was helping others exit through a window in one of the apartments. When Joanne and the girls got out of the building they saw others standing around; most were in some state of shock. Although the electricity was out, the sun was coming up; it was beginning to get light. It took nearly thirty minutes before the first emergency vehicles started to arrive. Apparently the damage was widespread. Joanne, her daughters, and the others who escaped the building were escorted to a temporary shelter in a park just a few blocks away. Later they were moved to a more permanent shelter.

Joanne had remained particularly calm during the entire episode, even when she couldn't get a response from Rosa. In a later conversation in the shelter Joanne explained that during the earthquake she had recalled two earthquakes in Mexico when she was a child, in one, the brick building she was in collapsed partially. Like this earthquake, she had to crawl out of that building as well. She had remained calm the first time by telling herself to stay calm and be patient. This time, she had also talked herself through it; she had told herself that she made it through the first one and could make it through this one as well. She said that knowing she had to take care of her daughters also helped her to stay calm. She also prayed.

Preparing Physically for Disaster

One of the major contributors to fear and panic is having to face the unknown. Any new experience that is unexpected will create anxiety. When the reaction to that anxiety is negative, people move easily into panic. And when people panic, they lose touch with their own personal resources and often end up making a bad situation worse. It is very important not to panic.

When disaster strikes, people can be thrown into a new physical environment that seems strange. They may be trapped in a small space; they may have to crawl on their hands and knees; they may have to run or climb; they may have to lift heavy objects or help carry someone to safety. They may be exposed to heat, cold, wetness, or wind, without being prepared. Survivors of disaster can easily find themselves suddenly in the dark; having to swim; or having to move themselves while injured.

Most younger children are used to running, jumping, and climbing. They can bend, twist, and roll on the ground. If they fall while they are playing they are able to get back up quickly.

Many adults, however, have gotten away from such activity and can find themselves physically underprepared during a disaster. On the other hand, children may not be as used to being in the dark, riding in an emergency vehicle, waiting in a strange place, handling the heat or cold, or being around people who are injured or possibly dead. There are benefits and drawbacks both for adults and for children.

In disasters people are hit by flying objects. They may fall to the ground or be trapped underneath an object. The more familiar with these unusual situations and the more physically fit people are, the better their chances of survival. Remember, familiarity gives one a sense of predictability, which, in turn, gives one a sense of control and reduces panic.

Physical Conditioning

Everyone is aware that of the importance of physical fitness, but what many don't realize is that being physically fit may save their lives and the lives of others during a disaster. If a piece of furniture falls on you, and no help is available for a period of time, removing it may be entirely up to you. Removing pieces of furniture and attempting to pry open doors that are stuck may take a good deal of muscle power. You may have to lift a heavy object off one of your family members in an emergency. If you are not used to walking long distances, but your car is stuck under a tree, you may find you have to push yourself. In earthquake drills children are taught to "duck and cover." When was the last time you tried to get under a table quickly? Imagine doing that at a restaurant. Imagine yourself "ducking and covering" at a movie theater, department store, or supermarket. When was the last time you had to crawl on your hands and knees, climb a tree, or carry your child a long distance? Clearly, good physical fitness becomes very important in a disaster.

Your physical fitness should include three basic areas, namely, strength, flexibility, and endurance. There are some general guidelines to starting any kind of exercise program: Start easy, don't strain. Build gradually, you're not in a race. Do it consistently. If you think you have any kind of physical problem, consult your physician before beginning. There are also numerous videotapes, health clubs, and commercial exercise programs available to assist you, not to mention what is readily available on television.

Exercises for Strength

1. Do push-ups, sit-ups, and deep knee bends.
2. Walk up and down stairs, or a nearby hill.
3. Lift and carry several books, keeping your back straight.
4. Sitting beneath a desk or table, try pulling yourself up (pull-up).
5. Interlocking your hands, pull or push from opposite directions (isometrics).

Strength-Building Game

For children 5 to 10 years of age or for children who will understand and cooperate.

Parents say:

"In this game there are several things to do. It is like an obstacle course and it will make you stronger. Are you ready? Do the things I do."

1. Do one or more pushups. (All exercises depend on what you and the child can do.)
2. Do one or more sit-ups.
3. Do one or more deep knee bends.
4. Lift and carry several books or some object weighing several pounds.
5. Sit underneath a table or desk and try pulling yourself up.
6. Interlock your hands, pull or push from opposite directions.
7. If you have stairs where you live, walk up and down the stairs (or a nearby hill) and then return home.

As the children learn the game add timing to see who gets done first. Increase the number of repetitions as the children get faster at completing the series. Add new strength-building tasks as you go along. Set an attainable goal for each child with some reward for reaching that goal.

Exercises for Flexibility

1. Yoga and Tai Chi Chuan are probably the best exercises for developing flexibility. They also develop strength, balance, and mental and emotional calm.
2. While sitting on the floor, keep your legs straight and bend forward slowly. Try to touch your toes. Repeat the exercise several times, stretching a little more each time.
3. Lie on your back and raise your knees over your head, stretching your lower back.
4. Lie on your stomach. Try to raise just your head and shoulders by placing your hands underneath your shoulders and lifting. This will arch your back.
5. While standing, bend to the left and lift your right arm over your head. Then bend to the right and lift your left arm over your head.
6. While standing, extend your arms and twist right and left.
7. While siting or standing, practice rotating your head slowly in all directions in order to stretch your neck.

Flexibility Game

Parents say:

"In this game there are seven things to do. There is a reward for those who improve doing these fun exercises. Are you ready? Do the things I do!" Increase the time playing this game as the children improve. Be sure to add a reward that is meaningful to the child.

1. Look at a book on Yoga or Tai Chi Chuan and have the children do one or more simple flexibility exercises.
2. Sit on the floor. Keep your legs and back straight and slowly bend forward. Try to touch your toes. If you can't do it perfectly that okay. Try it several times stretching a little more each time.
3. Lie on your back and raise your knees over your head, stretching you lower back.
4. Lie on your stomach. Try to raise just your head and shoulders by placing your hands underneath your shoulders and lifting.
5. Stand up. Bend to the left and lift your right arm over your head. Now bend to the right and lift your left arm over your head. Now put your arm down.

6. Now put your arms up and to your side and twist first right, then left.
7. Now move your head first left, then right, then back, then to the front.

Exercises for Endurance
1. All aerobic exercises will build endurance. Running, walking, hiking, jogging in place, biking, swimming, or playing any active sport for at least twenty minutes, three times a week, will build endurance.
2. Walking up and down stairs for twenty minutes, several times a week will help build endurance.
3. There are numerous exercise videos that help you to build aerobic endurance safely.
4. Regularly play active sports or games, such as tag or chase, with your children.

Endurance Game
There are numerous aerobic exercises which will be beneficial. Choose one or more from the list given and make a race out of it. Or play an active game with your children such as tag, throwing basketballs or throwing a ball for a half hour. Combine several aerobic activities. Plan a picnic at the end of a hike. Plan a reward for the person who gets back to the car first.

Have the family watch a join in an exercise video on a daily basis. Change the video often to keep up interest.

Preparing for Darkness

Although it is easy to recommend having a flashlight to see in the dark, people need also be prepared for the event that they don't have a flashlight or the flashlight malfunctions. For example, what happens if you're nowhere near your house or car and the power goes out at night? If no flashlight is available, are there candles to use? If not, are there matches nearby, or emergency lights that only go on when the electricity goes off? Perhaps you can make a fire, but can you do it safely? Obviously, the first line of defense is having safety lights of some kind. But alternatives must also be planned for when these helpful devices are not available.

Here are a few things you can do

1. Once a month have the whole family spend thirty minutes in the house with all the lights off. See if you could eat a meal together. See if you and the children can find your way through all the rooms in the house. You might want to play a game of "hide and seek," but don't make it scary.
2. You might take the family on a nighttime walk around your neighborhood (assuming that it is safe).
3. Just sitting with a child in his or her room for twenty to thirty minutes with all the lights off, talking, telling stories (not scary), or telling jokes can be helpful.
4. It is important for children to learn how to be by themselves in the dark. They can learn by playing games. For example, ask them to stay in the room next to yours, count to ten, and then find you. Over a period of weeks or months you can slowly increase the time that the child is alone in the dark. Also, help children develop some games to play while alone in the dark.

If you have a child who is particularly afraid, start very slowly. You might start by being with the child and dimming the lights in his or her room. Gradually over several nights or weeks you can reduce the lights until they are off.

Darkness Game

In addition to the games already mentioned children love this game. First with the child blindfolded lay out several objects (between ten and twenty) of different sizes and shapes on a table.

Parents say:
"I want you to pick up each item and tell me what it is. Try to guess what it is a part of.

"What color do you think it is?"
Tell the child that there is a prize for guessing a certain number correct.

Preparing for Climate

When a disaster strikes you may suddenly find yourself and your children exposed to the weather. It may be hot, cold, wet, or dry.

And you may not be immediately prepared for the new conditions. Because you may have to wait until proper clothing or shelter can be provided, it is important that you and your children develop some physical tolerance for uncomfortable temperatures. Children especially are used to being protected and may be very intolerant when they are uncomfortable.

A note of caution: The practices themselves should not be life threatening! A change in body temperature of only one or two degrees is sufficient to make one feel uncomfortable. Very young children (under three years of age) and elderly adults should not be stressed very much. Individuals who are sick, have a heart condition, are pregnant, have asthma, or who have any other condition that warrants concern should not participate in such exercises.

Preparing for Intense Heat

1. Take a family camping trip to the desert during the summer.
2. Turn off the air conditioner or fan for one or two days during the summer or during a heat wave.
3. If you live in a cooler region, add more clothes than are necessary or turn the heat up five to ten degrees to the point where you are uncomfortable.

Preparations of this type should be done once a month for the first six months and then every three months thereafter. During these exercises children should be discouraged from excessive complaining, because in the event of a real emergency complaining will remind everyone of their discomfort and may reduce the will to survive. There will be plenty of time to complain later. You might explain to children that this is an exercise, not necessarily a fun family outing. You might also offer rewards for those who do not complain or for those who show cooperation and help during the exercise. Challenge the children to find some creative ways to make themselves comfortable without using something that might not be available during a disaster. It is important to learn how to communicate and get along with others while you are uncomfortable. Discomfort causes irritability and fighting which needs to be controlled during an emergency.

If you encounter a lot of resistance from the majority of family members, start off slowly by having shorter periods of practice (one to three hours). As the family develops more tolerance increase the time (twenty-four to forty-eight hours). Camping trips are ideal for this purpose.

Heat Remedies
1. Drink plenty of water. The water supports perspiration, the body's natural cooling mechanism.
2. Get near moving air. Take turns fanning each other slowly.
3. Limit or slow down physical activity. Physical activity generates heat.
4. Move toward shade. Move away from heat sources.
5. Move to lower areas; hot air rises.
6. Remove extra clothing.
7. Rest or sleep. The body temperature drops during sleep.

Preparing for Intense Cold
1. Go camping during the cooler months.
2. If you live near snow, take some hikes or have a picnic.
3. Turn down the heat in your house five or ten degrees during the winter months for a period of several hours or possibly for a couple of days on a weekend.
4. Bathe or shower in cold water.
5. Spend a couple of hours in your backyard on a cool evening without jackets or sweaters.

Please read the comments and cautions on page 43. Be sensible. Don't do any exercise that might encourage a child to get sick or endanger someone's safety.

Cold Remedies
1. Move closer to a heat source.
2. Get away from moving air.
3. Huddle close to others.
4. Look for clothes, blankets, or other material to cover yourself with. You want to contain your body heat.
5. Make sure your main torso and head are covered before your fingers and toes. Your core body heat is essential to avoid hypothermia.

6. Stay dry.
7. Move to higher areas. Hot air rises.
8. Stay active. Sing; move around; pace; play games; maintain a conversation or group discussion; and so on.
9. Drink warm or hot liquids.
10. Try to stay awake. If you have to sleep take short naps.

Hot and Cold Game

Ask the child or children sit with you. Say:

"Tell me all the things you could do to make yourself cooler if it was very hot." or

"Tell me all the things you could do to make yourself warmer if it was very cold."

Tell the children to pretend that the heater and cooler did not work in the house. Give a small reward to the child who can repeat the most things to do, or the most original thing to do in these situations.

Preparing for Wetness

1. Take a family walk in the rain (if there is no lightning or thunder). Don't wear a raincoat or use an umbrella.
2. Wearing your regular clothes, have a water fight in the back yard on a sunny day. Stay wet for a couple of hours. Let yourself air dry.
3. Play in a wading pool with your clothes on. Be sure the smallest child can easily stand above the water line.

Please read the comments and cautions on page 43. Be sensible. Don't do any exercise that might encourage a child to get sick or endanger someone's safety.

Wetness Remedies

1. Remove as many wet clothes as feasible, but not if you will become colder. It is safer to be wet and warm than it is to be dry and cold. If your clothes are made from wool they will retain the heat even if they are wet.
2. Move closer to a heat source for drying.
3. Get near moving air for faster drying.

Preparing for Dryness
1. Abstain from all liquids for twenty-four hours (not for the young, sick, or elderly).
2. Take a desert vacation or camping trip.

Dryness Remedies
1. Drink plenty of water.
2. Avoid drinking alcohol.
3. Eat fruit or vegetables with high water content (cucumbers, lettuce, tomatoes, carrots).
4. Wear wet clothing (hat, scarf, T-shirt, and so on).
5. Use skin cream or lip balm.
6. Move out of the wind.
7. Move into shade.

Remember, heat and cold are more critical factors for safety than wet or dry.

In your disaster kits there should be clothing or an emergency blanket that can retain or reflect heat as well as protect you from rain. A change of clothing and an emergency blanket can be easily stored in a small bag and placed in the trunk of your car.

Please read the comments and cautions on page 43. Be sensible. Don't do any exercise that might encourage a child to get sick or endanger someone's safety.

Social and Environmental Preparation for Disaster

One of the most positive aspects of learning about disasters is learning that no one is alone. Whether the disaster is personal, human-made, or natural makes no difference. In any disaster children instinctively look to parents for help and parents can look to family, friends, the local or state community, and sometimes the federal government.

Which Family Members Can You Count On?

Most people can count on their spouse to contact them in a disaster. For those who are single or whose spouse cannot immediately contact them, however, it is helpful to have a network of family members. This should include individuals in the local area as well as those who live out of state.

In the California earthquake of January 1994, it was not possible to call parts of certain cities, but it was possible to call out of state. Dr. Deskin was able to phone his brother in Florida to get in contact with his son in Santa Barbara. His brother had agreed to be the contact point for the family. That is, if it was not possible to contact one another, they agreed to leave messages in Florida for each other. This arrangement of using an out-of-state relative or friend appears to work well most of the time—it is unlikely that all parts of the country would be suffering from the same disaster at the same time.

Those who have family members they can depend on in an emergency are fortunate. Making arrangements in advance or at least discussing the possibility of this kind of assistance allows them to feel more secure. Remember, this type of help usually lasts a short time. Within a few hours it will likely be possible to get help from others in the community.

The Neighborhood Watch

The Neighborhood Watch is a popular concept in many suburban communities throughout the United States. It usually involves designating one house in the neighborhood a safe house where children can go if they need protection and their parents are not home. The concept was originally designed to help prevent crime in neighborhoods. In many cases, though, parents pitch in to store additional food, water, blankets, and emergency supplies at a specified neighbor's house. Oftentimes these designated houses are registered with the local fire department as a place where people will gather in case of an emergency.

Safety in Numbers

Most often a small group of people can work as a team to provide a more thorough response in an emergency. Some people can tend to the injured while others gather material and still others try to establish communication with emergency personnel. The sayings Many hands make light work, and Two heads are better than one, often prove true in an emergency.

Suggestions

1. Designate a place where family members will meet in the event of a disaster. Designate a place in your home or on your property, and also a place in your neighborhood, where you will meet in case your property is destroyed
2. Have a designated person or family you will call in the event of a disaster. That person, or family, can relay messages to other family members. It is important to have at least two contact people: one who is local and one who is out of state.
3. Through your local fire department locate the nearest shelters in your area. Pay them a visit so you are familiar with several routes to get there. Take your children and show them so that they are familiar with the surroundings.
4. Make contact with the school and ask them where they take children in the event that they have to evacuate the building in an emergency. Visit that place with your children.
5. If there are no designated shelters in your area, it is important to know that rescue teams like to set up temporary shelters in school auditoriums, church halls, and larger public buildings that may be centrally located. If you are caught in a disaster you may have to make your way to one of these facilities.

Preparation for Safety Issues

How Well Do You Know Your Environment?

In any disaster, safety is the primary issue. As many people know, the majority of accidents occur in people's own home. Usually, these accidents are minor. In a major disaster, however, where electricity is cut off and people are in the dark or semi-dark, it is important to know where potentially life-saving objects are.

1. Do you have a fire extinguisher at home?
2. Do you know where the fire extinguishers are at your place of employment and your home?

3. Do you know where the fire alarms are where you work or shop?
4. When you go to bed can you easily find a flashlight?
5. Are your slippers or shoes always easy to find in the middle of the night?
6. If you live in a cold region and something happens to your house such as a fire or earthquake, do you have a set of clothes in your car or someplace outside of your house?

These are just some examples of the crises that may occur because you haven't adequately prepared for emergencies.

How Safe Is Your House?

Whether they live in earthquake country or hurricane country, most people consider their home a safe place, a nest, a place of comfort. But when people are unprepared, that nest can become a trap.

For example
1. Is your house bolted to its foundation? Can your roof withstand a strong hurricane?
2. Is your house adequately fireproofed?
3. Is your house adequately insulated so you can survive the cold if your heater fails?
4. Do you have a picture or mirror hanging over your or your children's beds? Are they on double hooks or bolted to the wall so they cannot fall?
5. Are the bookcases or bureau in your bedroom bolted to the wall so they won't fall on you or block the doorway?
6. If you live in an area where things fall, are your pictures covered with glass, or unbreakable glass or plastic?
7. Do you have safety lights and/or flashlights in every room, so that if something happens in the middle of the night you can see where everything and everyone is?
8. Are you sure everyone's nightclothes, especially your children's, are fire retardant?

Where Are the Safe Areas in the Buildings You Spend Time in?

Most people move from home to an office or other building during the day. If they are not working, they may be at shopping centers, department stores, doctors' offices, and so on. Yet if asked where they should go or what they should do in a fire, earthquake, or other disaster, most would not know the answer. Most large buildings post clear notices not to use the elevator in case of fire and large exit signs at stairways. But some smaller, older buildings posts no safety signs at all. It is up to you to notice where the stairways are in any building you enter. In schools children are taught emergency and fire drills about where to go and what to do. This may help to keep them as safe as possible.

Where Should Your Children Go If Disaster Strikes When You Are Not There?

As mentioned above, schools have an excellent program to protect children while they are at school, but what about after school, or in the evening? Parents should make up their own drills at home so that children know exactly what to do if there is a fire at home or in any building they are in during the day.

Where Should Your Children Go and What Should They Do at Night?

Although parents are normally home at night when a disaster strikes they may not be able to contact their children. For example, a fire in a hallway may prevent parents from coming to their child's assistance. In an earthquake with furniture moving around and doors becoming stuck parents may not be able to immediately help their children. Children need to know what to do in advance so they automatically do it correctly. For example, exiting through a window, if it is safe to do so, may be the first thing a child should do. Checking their bedroom door to see if smoke is coming through the bottom might prevent them from opening the door and being in greater danger suddenly. Whatever the safest method, children should be taught in advance how to exit their rooms.

Take Time to Notice or Ask

Home Environment

1. If there was a flood in your neighborhood, from what direction would it most likely come and where would it go? Which streets would most likely get flooded first? What would be the safest escape routes? Take the time now to think ahead.

2. Which way does the wind usually blow? In the event of a fire, where would it most likely start and in which direction would it travel? Which roads might be blocked off? Visit your local library and check into the records of fires, floods, hurricanes, tornadoes, or other disasters in your area. Notice where they happen most frequently.

3. If you live near a coastal region, which are the best routes to move inland?

Work Environment

1. Locate the fire extinguishers, stairways, and fire alarms in your building. In larger buildings the fire extinguishers and alarms are often in the same area on each floor.

2. If you had to leave the building in a hurry, what route would you use? If that route was blocked, is there an alternate route?

3. If you had to break a window, is something available to break it with?

Restaurants, Department Stores, Movie Theaters, and Other Buildings

1. Whenever you enter any building for the first time, take a few minutes to look around. Notice where the location of exits. Look for fire extinguishers and fire alarms. If the building is two or more stories, locate the stairways. All of this can be done casually without drawing attention to yourself. In some cases you can ask your children to find as many of these items as they can. They may think it is a fun game.

Preparation for Adequate Communication

How and When Do You Contact the Police or Fire Department?

In an emergency, parents should first ensure the safety of their family, and then call 911. If the lines are blocked, which sometimes happens in a large emergency, parents should be prepared for that. Locate a cellular phone, if one is available. If not, don't panic. Most cities have a coordinated disaster response system in place for large emergencies. A good example is the Oklahoma City explosion in 1995. Within a very short time help was organized by a number of city, state, federal, and even private agencies to help victims and their families. Both police and fire departments in most cities can locate and contact the appropriate agencies that provide the type of help needed if they themselves do not offer that help. For example, police departments will know the location of shelters set up by the Red Cross or other agencies.

How Can Your Children Find You in the Dark?

If the electricity fails and no light is available, children may not be able to find their parents. Making simple preparations so that children know what to do in such an emergency can be helpful. Providing a whistle with its own distinctive sound to every member of the household would be useful. Or assigning each family member a specific code would simplify the task of identifying everyone and finding his or location. For example, if father's code was one short blast of the whistle, mother's, two short blasts, and so on, it would be easy to know where everybody was.

The Advantages of Communication Devices

Whistles and flashlights are both useful for close communication. But what about distant communication, when the phone lines are down? Beepers and cellular telephones have been very useful in many disasters. Unfortunately, cellular phones are expensive to maintain, but they are becoming cheaper all the time. And in a disaster, they may be one of few options available for communicating with loved ones. Walkie-talkies, which have a range of up to five miles, are another good option. If family members are separated, which can happen for a variety of reasons, they can use walkie-talkies to stay in contact. CB radios, if the electricity is on or if run by batteries, are another alternative for communicating at longer distances. And most likely, other options would work in certain situations. The most important thing is that people have access to communication when they are in need.

Flares, Fires, Smoke, and Rock Signals

When electronic devices are not available, other, traditional methods of communication may be the only option. Flares are good, both at night and during the day, for signaling low-flying rescue teams. A fire, too, if it can be made safely out in the open, can help rescuers locate missing people. When in thicker or wooded areas, however, smoke may be more visible. Smoke can be created by placing some damp leaves on a small fire. Smoke signals, made by fanning a blanket or broad, large leaves, is another signal for help. The universal sign for help is three small smoke clouds followed by three larger clouds, and then three smaller clouds. And finally, spelling out SOS with rocks is a good option in areas of higher visibility.

Materials to Bring and Ways to Prepare for a Disaster

The type of disaster determines what materials are needed. Disasters range from personal, which affect one person, to major, which affect a whole city or select area. Below are lists of materials needed for a variety of disasters, as well as activities that could result in disaster.

A long hike in the woods

energy snacks, and water if the hike will last several days
orange or yellow plastic garbage bags (to prevent hypothermia and help rescuers find you)

pocket knife
a whistle for each member of the party
a compass, with knowledge about how to use it
a reflector or hand mirror
insect repellent
medical supplies, such as a tube of antibiotic ointment and
    plastic bandage strips
suntan lotion, sunglasses or any other seasonal supplies
essential medication
waterproof matches in a waterproof container
appropriate clothing for both day and night

Car Trips during the Winter
What to Check
travel advisory messages
oil, to be sure it appropriate for winter conditions
antifreeze level
ignition system
battery
lights
heating and cooling system
fuel and fuel system
brakes
windshield wipers
defroster
tires—are snow tires necessary?
radio

What to Bring
cellular phone, if available
winter emergency travel kit
several blankets, or several orange or yellow garbage bags to
    prevent hypothermia
shovel
sand
tow chain
flashlight
compass
several warning lights or road flares
water and energy snacks

ax, or hatchet
booster cables
ice scraper
first-aid kit
essential medication
matches in a waterproof container
travel fire extinguisher
methyl hydrate (for fuel line and windshield de-icing)
small, battery-powered radio, with spare batteries
road maps

Floods

1. Shut off electricity or power. Do not stand in water while doing this. If standing in water is unavoidable, however, use a dry stick or rubber covered tool to turn off the switch.
2. Turn off the gas at the outside meter.
3. Use bottled water or add two drops of bleach per liter or quart of tap water thirty minutes before drinking.
4. Have a working portable radio with spare batteries.
5. Keep emergency food, water, medical supplies, and clothing on hand, in a safe, readily accessible place in an upper level, or in the car if evacuation is the plan.
6. Move keepsakes and valuable items to a higher level in the house.
7. Discard weed killers, insecticides, and so on, to prevent pollution.
8. If possible, remove toilet bowls and plug basement sewer drains and toilet connections with wooden plugs.
9. If evacuation is necessary (usually in the case of floods, fires, hurricanes, and chemical spills), bring the following:
   battery-powered radio and spare batteries
   flashlight for each person
   warm clothing and blankets
   essential medicines and infant-care items
   personal toiletries
   emergency supplies
   identification for each member, especially children
   vital personal and family documents

The Ideal Survival Kit

When putting together survival kits, one needs to consider two possible results of a disaster. In some disasters such as hurricanes and some earthquakes people are unable to stay in their own homes. They then have to consider needs for warmth, and for food and drink, as well as other basic supplies. If one's home is demolished, one also needs to consider shelter as well as provisions for warmth and protections from the elements, such as rain.

The materials a family would bring on, say, a two-week camping trip constitute the ideal survival kit. Although this example may seem farfetched, many disasters can totally destroy a home. Consider the devastation tornadoes, hurricanes, earthquakes, and fires leave in their path. It's best to be prepared for the worst, which can involve needing even the most basic necessities. Here is a list that attempts to encompass what is needed most. Add to this list your special needs such as special medications, toiletries, and so on. Answer the question, "What would I want if I had to live in a tent for two weeks?"

a tent (if you had to evacuate your home)
a cooking stove with fuel, or other source of heat for cooking
adequate food and water
medical supplies, including special needs for the ill or elderly
season-appropriate clothing
flashlights or lanterns, and candles
matches
toiletries
a water purifier and water carriers such as gallon jugs
sleeping bags for the family
a portable radio with extra batteries
a crowbar, folding shovel, and camper saw
a manual can opener
plastic plates, cups, knives, forks, and spoons
a campers cooking set
emergency tools
a large empty and clean plastic garbage can to store these
materials
other items needed to live comfortably

Remember that by preparing in advance you can make individual changes that fit your needs and situation to modify this list. Help may or may not come quickly in a disaster. If you prepare adequately in advance your needs will be met.

4
True Stories: The Shaking Earth

Christopher Byron and his wife, Mary, lived in their first house in Northridge, a suburb of Los Angeles in the San Fernando Valley. Their three children, Mark, age eight, Elliot, age seven, and Joan, age five, all attended the local public school. Chris worked as an accountant for a large firm in Los Angeles. Mary had her hands full at home, with three children and taking care of the home. She was considering getting back into teaching, now that her youngest child was in kindergarten. Like many parents in the San Fernando Valley, the Byrons had made limited preparations for the possibility of an earthquake. Everyone knew that a large earthquake was probable, but, of course, no one knew when it would happen. The family kept a small supply of water and food, blankets, a battery-powered radio, several flashlights, and a first-aid kit in a plastic trash can in the garage.

At 4:30 a.m. Mary was awakened by a frightening sound. At first she could not place the sound or where it was coming from. It was like a bad movie with grinding, crunching. and roaring. As Chris awakened, the house began to shake. Suddenly, simultaneously, both realized it was another earthquake. They looked upward. Was this the big one? Will the roof come down? With every shaking movement their anxiety rose. They both felt they were going to die. The feeling of doom was temporarily lifted by an overwhelming concern for their children.

The roof had not yet fallen in on the house, but a small book-case had fallen on Mary's side of the bed. Neither Mary nor Chris could see what had fallen on her, but were both relieved that it had only knocked the breath out of her. The shaking continued, and Chris's bureau began to slide forward. Amidst the darkness and movement, all they could hear were pictures falling, furniture falling, mirrors falling. It was as though every furnishing was trying to lay flat on the floor.

Then they heard the children. It is extremely difficult to move around during an earthquake. But in a dark room, with fallen furniture blocking the path, it is impossible. Somehow Chris managed to reach his bureau and grab a flashlight. Luckily, the batteries worked. In the light's beam was another bureau that had slid in front of the door leading to the hallway. One minute had elapsed since the house first started shaking. Just as he moved toward the obstruction, the house stopped shaking. Mary screamed as she rushed to the door to help her husband move the bureau out of the way. The children's screams were now frantic.

The next hurdle was the bedroom door. The house had moved about an eighth of an inch, enough to jam the door enough that they couldn't pull it open. Fortunately, Chris had placed a crowbar in his closet, just in case. As he pried it open, they both looked out into the hallway. The electricity was out, but the flashlight illuminated pieces of glass from family pictures that had fallen and shattered. He immediately called to the children, "We're coming!" and he and Mary put on slippers. Avoiding glass with each step, they slowly made their way into each child's room. The boys shared a room, luckily, and were trying to support each other. As Chris made his way over to them, Mary rushed to Joan's room, scooping her out from her bed, where she was huddled under the covers. Pictures lay shattered on the floor, including those that were hung over the bed. Mirrors had fallen and cracked. Every piece of tall furniture, including a bookcase, had fallen over. But nothing had fallen on the children.

Chris and Mary embraced their children, while simultaneously rushing them to put on their shoes and warning them to be careful of glass. But by this time Mark had already stepped on a piece of glass and was bleeding quite severely. All three children were sobbing; their parents were not far from it. After checking inside and outside the house for cracks and structural damage, Chris decided that the house was structurally sound, for the moment. He could not smell gas and the water lines appeared to be intact. In the meantime, Mary went to the garage for the first-aid kit and stopped the bleeding on Mark's foot. They began to fill the bathtub with water, in case all water was going to be cut off, and attended to holding and reassuring their children that everything was going to be fine.

Lighting a camping lantern and some candles around the house provided enough light to bundle up in warm clothes and boots. All the while, Chris and Mary were talking to the children, assigning them duties to help and inspecting the bathrooms and kitchen. Fortunately, they had locking cupboards so their dishes and glassware did not fall out, but the glass cabinet in the dining room had fallen over, breaking some of their crystal. By the time the lights came on, Chris and Mary had swept up most of the glass and put their house back into some order.

They were lucky. The cracks in the house were small and not dangerous. Their house had withstood the shock, and they were all physically fine, with the exception of Mark's foot. The roads were mostly clear so they could get to the doctor. Fortunately, telephone service was restored quickly for part of the city. They used their cellular phone to call the doctor to make sure he would be in. Although markets in the area were closed, they had enough food and water for several days. The gas was shut off, but they could use their camping stove to heat water and cook. For the children it was just like camping out. Once they had attended to the safety of their children and home, Mary and Chris phoned their parents to let them know they and the children were fine.

Chris realized later that he had overlooked several important items in his preparation for an earthquake. He hadn't installed emergency lights that would come on when the electricity went out. He hadn't realized that in earthquake country no pictures or mirrors should be above a bed unless they were secured at all four corners so they couldn't fall. He hadn't thought about bolting furniture to the wall. But after everything was considered, he was extremely happy he had done as much as he did. He realized he could have been better prepared, but counted his blessings, made the necessary repairs and installed better earthquake safeguards, and went on to restore order to his life and his home. Sunday morning the entire family dressed, went to church, and went out for their usual Sunday lunch. The Byrons realized that the best thing for them, and especially for the children, was to get back to their usual routine.

Once the dust settled and the physical problems were taken care of for the present, however, it became clear that all members of the family were still experiencing certain aftereffects. Nobody wanted to sleep in their own bedroom. Nobody wanted to sleep alone. Whenever a car, and certainly a truck, went by, everybody tensed up as the house shook. It was as though they were all waiting, ready for the next shock. The children alternated between clinging and demanding behavior, and irritability and fighting with one another. Chris and Mary lived with a daily fear that it would happen again. When they discussed these fears with each other and with friends, they found they were not alone. A local clinic was offering counseling to help people cope with the effects of the earthquake. The whole family attended. After several weeks they began to feel better. They learned that it was normal for their children to want to sleep in their parents' room, and that it was okay to allow that. After some time, the children agreed to sleep together in one room; eventually, Joan went back to her own room.

Although neither wanted to go through an earthquake again, Chris and Mary both felt they had learned something. They could work together and trust each other. Surviving the disaster made them feel stronger and more confident they could handle the next, if one should occur. They are also better prepared for an emergency than they once were.

5
What to Do during a Disaster

Knowing what to do when disaster strikes greatly enhances the chances for survival. While some (mostly weather-related) disasters come with warning, many do not. Earthquakes, landslides, house fires, and vehicle accidents usually provide little warning. Proper responses to disaster can be broken down into three separate phases, each a little different, depending upon the type of disaster, but each designed to maximize the chance for survival, both for oneself and his or her family. What is proper depends in part on one's location at the time, such as at home, the office, a store, and so on. For our purposes, we will assume the event happens while its victims are at home.

Emergency Phase One: The First Few Moments

With advance warning, people can prepare by securing their home and leaving the area, taking with them everything necessary for survival, such as medication, irreplaceable belongings, vital documents, photo albums, food, milk, water, pets and their food, and so on. But what about disasters that strike with no warning? In these types of disaster, including earthquakes, land-slides, house fires, and others, people have little or no warning, and the initial danger period is usually over very quickly.

Time is crucial. The first thing to do is identify what is happening or what has just happened, because different disasters require different responses. If people are prepared, they will be able to identify what is happening more quickly, and take action to ensure the safety of themselves and their children. Reports of disorientation or confusion are common at this point. This is one of the reasons planning is so important.

Almost simultaneously, take stock of your own physical safety. Are you hurt? Trapped? In need of something? Check on other family members, as well. It is best to plan ahead of time how and in what order to help them. Ideally, each person has learned what role he or she will play. Another important point: Always assess the danger to yourself when helping someone else. You'll do no one any good if you hurt yourself. Move quickly, but not so quickly that you lose sight of the situation and potential hazards.

Finally, evaluate the environment for further physical damage. For example, nothing may have fallen on anyone yet, but it may soon. Or, in the case of an earthquake, prepare for a major after-shock. It may be necessary to evacuate the family to a safe area selected beforehand.

Emergency Phase Two: Evaluation and Action

Clearly, these phases do not always neatly fall into categories, but rather, overlap. After conducting a rapid safety check in the first phase, make a more thorough passing, checking family members for injury and the surroundings for any danger. For example, is anything burning? Should the electricity be turned off? Does anyone smell gas? Is some area of the house flooding? Should the water be turned off? Is anyone seriously hurt or bleeding? With what types of injuries? If evacuation is necessary, can those who are injured be moved? In the event that someone has a spinal injury or broken bones, would it be more dangerous to leave them where they are or to move them? Making no decision because of uncertainty may be the wrong decision. And finally, especially if someone is hurt, is help accessible? Are phone lines down? Is a cellular phone available? How about a neighbor?

Evaluate the psychological health of everyone involved. First, ask questions; second, observe them. Children as well as spouses may need to be held and comforted. Remember, too, that shock often leaves people unable to talk or communicate their feelings.

Next, respond with action. In a house fire, the best action is to move the family to safety and then call 911. The first phase lasts minutes; this phase, hours or days. Adjust the response accordingly. For example, if during this phase everyone is safe, it may be wise to check on neighbors or others in the area to see how they are. Many report that time seems to move slowly during a disaster, but in actuality, events occur within seconds. It is interesting how much detail, especially the sequence of events, people can recall immediately after an accident. Some report seeing everything in slow motion.

Most disasters take place within seconds. It is important to remember that if you've survived the initial impact, you will likely survive the entire event. But that realization, while comforting in one sense, cannot take over. The second emergency phase is still dangerous and requires calmness, clarity, and the proper response.

Emergency Phase Three: What to Do Next

The following is a partial recap of the phases above, but more detailed. The assumption is, it is now a few minutes into the disaster. You are out of danger, if possible, and have made the initial physical and emotional evaluation.

What Should You Do Mentally during a Disaster?

1. Identify what has happened, and estimate the severity of the incident. For example, a house fire may require one

set of actions, while an earthquake with an expected after-shock may require another course of action.

2. Recall your emergency plans. Ask yourself the following:
   Where am I supposed to go?
   Where are my alternative places to stay?
   Where are my emergency supplies?
   Whom should I contact?
   What local, city, state, or federal agencies will give assistance?
   What kind of help do I need most, right now?
   Use codes to help you remember—for example, DAC for "duck and cover."

3. Focus on the plan. Do not start imagining worst-case scenarios. If others are involved, especially children, keep them focused on the present. Tell them they will have plenty of time later to worry or grieve. Keep them alert and clear-headed.

4. Recall past experiences in which you were successful under pressure.

5. Be patient. It may take time for help to arrive. Use relaxation techniques, such as taking deep breaths, to keep focused and clear headed. One relaxation procedure is included in appendix B.

6. Remember that most people are rescued within hours, or within one or two days. If you have to wait, prepare yourself mentally.

7. If waiting for help to arrive, remember that sound, smoke, and light will aid the rescuers in finding you.

8. Continually reassess the situation. What else can be done? Has anything been overlooked?

9. Assess your emotional well-being and that of your family. How is everyone coping? Keep in mind that children cope with crises situations differently than adults. Check children for signs of problems. Watch for less-obvious signs, too, such as a child withdrawing, or being unusually quiet. Children do not have the resources to handle the enormous psychological stress that a disaster presents, so they will need additional support.

10. Prevent fear, sadness, or thoughts of failure by keeping

your mind active. Use an approach that has helped you before—for example, prayer, games, recollection of positive events in your life, or any activity that will lessen fear or sadness.

11. Avoid blaming. Blame and finger-pointing can damage the morale of even a small group.

12. Remember that it is normal to be afraid in a fearful situation, although it may not be helpful to express it.

What Should You Do Emotionally during a Disaster?

There is time after a disaster to make decisions and deal with feelings and emotions. During a disaster, however, especially one that lasts only seconds, there is not time to sort out all the conflicting emotions that emerge—emotions such as grief, anger, sadness, aloneness, and the need to exercise patience and control. Controlling feelings during a disaster may mean the difference between life and death. If feelings are too overwhelming, making life-saving decisions is extremely difficult, if not impossible.

Children will often exhibit the same symptoms during a disaster that they exhibit afterwards. They may have difficulty sleeping, or nightmares about frightening things such as ghosts and monsters. They may relive the terrifying experience over and over again. Children's memories of a disaster will usually emerge in their play. Or, in the height of the disaster, children may actually play to deal with their fear. Children may show difficulties concentrating, or become irritable and aggressive. They may not want to talk about the disaster, during or afterwards. Children take their cues from their parents. The degree of control a parent exhibits will affect how the child behaves.

One of the worst things that can happen during a disaster is losing a family member. Children deal differently with death, depending on several factors such as age and maturity. Parents may have to control and/or delay their grief to support their children and protect them from further harm.

What Should You Do Physically during a Disaster?

1. Execute the plan. The plan, especially if written out, will help you focus and remember important steps you may forget otherwise.
2. Get to safety. Distance yourself and your family from the source of danger. Make sure children do not explore potentially dangerous areas.
3. Use your senses. Look around. Could things fall on you? Are there cracks in the walls or ceilings? Do you need to be in a low area or a high area? Do you need to be near water, or in a dry area? Listen. Do you hear a hissing sound? Could it be a gas leak? Do you hear cracking sounds? Is something breaking? Do you hear running water? Do you hear the voices of others? Smell for odors. Do you smell smoke? Gas? Other noxious fumes?
4. Make yourself visible so that you can be rescued if that applies.
5. At the first opportunity, check yourself for injuries, bleeding, and broken bones. In the heat of the excitement, it is easy to miss an injury you'd ordinarily notice.
6. Check others for injuries. Save only those you can save. Call for help, if necessary.
7. Turn on the television, if possible, to get information about what to do, or who to call for help. Evaluate whether or not children should see what is being broadcast, however.
8. If your children are at school, the school may have its own disaster plan. Make sure your family is secure. And make sure the streets are safe before you pick them up.

What Materials Should You Gather?

1. Anything that distances you and your family from the source of danger. Your safety comes first.
2. Flashlights, mirrors, matches, flares, whistles, bells, pots and pans—anything that will get you noticed. Most rescue efforts take place within the first twenty-four to seventy-two hours, and human beings can live a few days without

water and a few weeks without food. Gather the emergency supplies you set aside previously, and anything else that will help rescue teams spot you. Sing if you feel it might help.

3. Any and all communication equipment. Battery-operated and CB radios, televisions, and a pair of walkie-talkies can be very useful. A cellular phone is indispensable. Even if lines are jammed, you will be able to get through at some point. Note: It may be easier to call out of the area to another state, or to have someone call in from another state, than it is to call locally. You should designate someone out of state whom all members of the family can contact in case of a disaster.

4. If outdoors, material to maintain your body temperature. In heat, get near water, wind, or shade, if possible. Remove clothing as needed. In cold, gather dry material that will retain heat. Move into the sunlight. Get out of the wind. If available, mud acts as an insulator and can be used to cover exposed limbs.

5. Water, if it is drinkable. If fire is accessible, boil the water to be sure.

6. Food supplies, as well as fuel, if there is a chance you will have to wait longer than a few hours. In such a case, develop a plan for rationing food.

What Should You Do with Others during a Disaster?

1. The number one rule: There is safety in numbers.
2. As soon as you are safe, gather family members, especially young children, or go to a predetermined meeting place.
3. Locate the nearest community shelter. They will have first aid, food, clothing, and communication devices. Rescue teams will contact the shelters first.
4. Groups of people are easier to locate than single individuals, and usually receive priority from rescue teams.

The Media

Having a radio or television during a disaster is usually a mixed blessing. Getting up-to-the-minute information and emergency instructions can be most helpful. The graphic images presented, however, particularly those shown on television that focus on the worst damage, can upset children. A portable radio with head-phones is the best option.

Some Final Notes

Events during a disaster can be extremely disorienting and con-fusing. They can happen quickly, or be drawn out for quite a while. While it is normal to feel a full range of emotions during a disaster, anger and irritability in particular must be contained during this phase. They aren't helpful; what's more, they could be harmful. Each member of the family, including the children, are potentially vital to the survival of the rest of the family.

Whenever possible, bring routines back to normal, quickly. The return to regular routines benefits children because it lessens their anxiety. Parents also feel better as their normal routine is reestablished.

6

Mental, Emotional, and Physical Reactions to Disaster

The Mental Effects of Disaster

The First Few Minutes

Reactions to disasters differ, depending upon various factors. People react differently in a hurricane, where they have hours or even days to prepare, than they do in an earthquake, which is often a complete surprise. Sometimes, the combination of shock, fear, helplessness, confusion, and anger, all occurring simultaneously, leave even the best-prepared unable to move.

People caught in disasters are often confused as to what to do first. They have to act quickly, but what should be done first?

People often try to sort out some meaning to what is happening, to place it in perspective. At the same time, they are grappling with their own fear of dying, or worse, not being able to help a loved one. Coupled with the strange sounds, smells, and tastes that often accompany disaster, acting in a logical and sensible way may be very difficult, unless they are physically, mentally, and emotionally prepared. In the earthquake of 1994 in Los Angeles, for example, people reported that the worst parts, initially, were the dark and the loud, eerie sounds the earthquake made, not the actual shaking.

Whether paralyzed, screaming hysterically, or calm, it helps to be aware that any and all reactions are normal, including the heroic impulse to jump in and save someone, as well as being critical of or angry at others. Most will be surprised by their own behavior. For example, many people who have acted heroically have said they just acted without thinking, and that if they had thought about it they may have behaved otherwise. Many are critical of their own cowardly behavior, but saving one's own life is instinctual. And by now, it should be clear: No one can help others until they first help themselves.

Even when the initial threat of disaster is over, or under control, the event is not over. The effects of a disaster, including flashbacks and certain types of posttraumatic stress, often stay with survivors for a long time.

Assuming one has dealt with the physical aspects, ensuring the family is safe, consider emotional reactions. Reassure family members with a supportive and positive tone. Keep them calm, and help them to start healing themselves. Knowing that someone is in control can also relieve and soothe family members. Healing continues as their world is put back together and seems manageable again. This may mean simply ensuring that each member of the family is adequately clothed and protected physically, or meeting their basic needs, such as food and water. With adequate preparation, and a little luck, meeting basic needs may not be too difficult.

After the Initial Shock

During the first few minutes, survival is the primary concern. After the initial shock, however, thoughts and questions about what happened and why arise. But spending too much time thinking about the disaster, rather than planning for the future, may not be helpful. The media frequently contributes to this problem, replaying the incident over and over. But this is the time to plan realistically for the immediate future—how to meet the physical and emotional needs of the family, how to find and secure a safe place. Now is the time to plan for the days ahead until the family can resume its normal routines. Now is not the time for blame. Being angry about lack of preparation does not help or solve anything; rather, it interferes with the family working together.

The Emotional Effects of Disaster

Shock, Numbness, or Terror

Feelings of shock or numbness, followed by terror or fear of dying, are normal reactions to any life-threatening situation. They can last only an instant, or a much longer period of time. These feelings are the body's way of gathering strength for the next step. When faced with danger it is normal to want to leave as soon as possible. For example, the instinctual response to being in a burning house is wanting to get out as quickly as possible. Another, almost instinctual, response is mentally assessing the situation. What happened? and What is going to happen? are the logical questions to ask before ascertaining what course of action to take.

Once the problem of physical safety is resolved it is important to release any pent-up feelings of anger, fear, sadness, guilt, love, gratitude, and happiness about having survived. People achieve this release by talking and sharing feelings. Communication with adults, as well as children, can also occur through touching, holding, and being close together to give support.

Anxiety and Fear

Most people regard anxiety and fear as negative emotions because they are painful. But these emotions play an immensely important role in people's lives by protecting them from harm. Once the initial shock of a disaster wears off, most people worry that it might happen again. But by taking control of a situation, it is possible to control feelings of panic, thereby reducing the level of anxiety. Taking the necessary steps to ensure one's personal safety, as well as the safety of loved ones, will achieve the sense of control. Reassuring others also helps to lower anxiety. There is something magical about holding a child and saying, "You are going to be all right, the worst is over," even when it may not be true. Children sense their parents' anxiety and worry. They respond by becoming anxious themselves. They may ask, "Are you afraid?" Answer them, truthfully, but tell them that the situation is going to improve. Be optimistic. This may become difficult as the family's emotional mood swings from joy that everyone is safe to grief and sadness about what was lost. The idea is to reduce feelings of panic and to allow the family to start working toward a positive recovery. As time passes and the family begins to heal, everyone will see that life is improving.

Reality Sets In

After a shock, people often take stock of their surroundings. For those that survived the Oklahoma City bombing or Hurricane Andrew, just to name a few, looking at their surroundings made them realize what could have happened. Some individuals become traumatized again by the devastation they see and the realization that they could have been hurt or killed.

Survival Guilt

As people view the devastation following a disaster and learn about the death of others, some of whom were close friends or relatives, they often ask, "Why me?" or "Why not me?" It is almost as though they feel they should have died, rather than those who did. This phenomenon has been reported by survivors of sunken ships, earthquakes, hurricanes, and numerous other disasters. It's called survival guilt, and is marked by depression and feeling unworthy of the gift of survival, as well as the notable absence of happiness. Survival guilt often disappears in time, but in those cases where it persists professional help should be sought.

Feeling Stuck, Trapped, or Isolated

Feelings of panic or anxiety are normal reactions to being trapped by falling debris or isolated in a room. The first thing to do is to free yourself, if you can. If not, let others know where you are. In most disasters, help is relatively near at hand. However, it may be minutes, hours, or even days before a rescue is completed. This is where preparation is most helpful. If you are trapped in a room, having a crowbar to pry open a door or a cellular phone to call out may be a lifesaver, or may at least reduce the time you are isolated and trapped. Having a whistle is also useful, since yelling may not be heard as readily and may strain, or damage, your voice. If you do call out, try to do so in a lower pitch. A lower pitch travels farther than a higher pitched voice.

Hysteria, or Lack of Control

Feelings of hysteria, and yelling and screaming are not uncommon in a disaster. They can be dangerous, however—not because of the act itself, but because becoming hysterical, or yelling and screaming do nothing to save yourself, or your children. In addition, hysterical behavior affects others, often leading to widespread fear and panic.

Abandonment, or Feeling Cut Off from Services

Most people are creatures of habit. They are used to listening to the radio, watching television, reading the newspaper, and talking to friends and family on the phone. When the electricity goes off, or if the roads are blocked, people are suddenly cut off from news, unless they have planned ahead, by including portable radios or televisions in their emergency kits. Even then, some stations may be unable to function if their electricity has been cut off.

This sudden lack of communication, coupled with the feeling that help will be slow in coming can lead to feelings of abandonment and isolation. These feelings are normal, and should be controlled by realizing that help will eventually arrive. Having a cellular phone on hand can help by enabling contact with others, a neighbor, loved one, or someone who can provide some support or comfort.

Worry about Loved Ones

Not knowing what happened to a loved one is often the scariest part of any disaster. Most parents become overwhelmed with anxiety when they are separated from their children. Keep in mind, most schools have plans in place to protect children in an emergency. Whether through fire drills, disaster preparedness, or other means, children are usually protected from harm. Unless a disaster strikes the school directly—a tornado, for example—children will probably be safe. Children should be taught the location of local police and fire stations, churches or synagogues, libraries, or other public places they can go in the event they are away from school and unable to get home. Again, planning ahead saves not only lives, but a great deal of anxiety. Having an out-of-state person to call when local phone lines are down may be useful in this regard as well.

Doom

When caught in a hurricane, earthquake, or other disaster, the possibility of death is real. Again, being prepared ahead of time can not only reduce that chance,but also reduce the fear associated with it. There are places that may not be entirely safe, but are definitely safer than standing in the middle of a room screaming. Depending on the type of disaster, getting to a doorway or under a solid table, away from overhead windows, or in a closet are only some of the alternatives. The act itself of protecting oneself or loved ones can greatly reduce the terrible fear of the unknown.

Stress and Posttraumatic Stress

Stress was addressed in an earlier chapter. If stress represents an unusual demand upon the mind and/or body, then stress is a normal partner to disaster.

Types of Stress Reactions to Disaster

Following a disaster, parents often show the symptoms of Acute Stress Disorder, which lasts from two days to four weeks. Not everyone will show the same symptoms, depending on personality or experience with stressful situations. Some may show signs of shock, numbness, or withdrawal. Some may walk around in a daze, not responding to those around them. Some may be unable to recall part of the disaster.

Others may have flashbacks or recurrent images, thoughts, or dreams of the disaster, reliving the experience when similar sounds or sights occur or somebody talks of that particular traumatic event. Many want to avoid anything that reminds them of it. These memories can affect sleep and concentration, and can produce irritability, restlessness, or increased anxiety. The aftereffects of shock can affect work or relationships with loved ones. In most cases, the worst of these symptoms are over within two to twenty-eight days. With time, most people are able to handle their feelings. Stress levels decrease as the symptoms abate.

For some people, however, these symptoms neither disappear nor improve, but continue to be disruptive. This condition, as defined earlier, is called Posttraumatic Stress Disorder.

The Effects of Posttraumatic Stress

When disaster strikes and the stress lasts more than three months it is called chronic posttraumatic stress. The symptoms are similar, but they differ in duration. Some individuals are so traumatized, so afraid that another life-threatening disaster will occur, that they are unable to let the feelings go. Symptoms may persist, eventually affecting everything—work, relationships, and so on. Adults tend to relive the experience over and over, or avoid everything that reminds them of the event. Many become irritable, have difficulty sleeping and concentrating, or have an exaggerated tendency to become startled. Depending on their age, children may show different symptoms, which may last for only a short time or for quite a while. These symptoms may include bed wetting, soiling, or whiny or clingy behavior. If symptoms persist beyond three months, you may need to consult a professional.

What Can You Do Physically After a Disaster?

Rest

Literature on disasters tells stories of individuals demonstrating amazing feats of physical strength or endurance. Sometimes human beings are able to do more than would seem physically possible. Along with this endurance or strength, however, may come the tendency to ignore oneself. Those trained in rescue techniques, or others who work in disasters are also trained not to overexert or overtire themselves. Parents need to understand that trying to be "Superparent" can lead to failure if they do not take care of their bodies with enough rest.

Eat Well

After a disaster there is so much to do that nutrition may not seem important. People eat junk food rather than their usual diet. They may drink more alcohol or skip meals. These practices quickly lead to burnout. It is vital that each member of the family, parent and child alike, is careful about what he or she eats and drinks. Nutritional needs may be more important following a disaster than before, since individuals are under more stress. Diet should be healthy—and as close to normal as possible—during and after a disaster.

Exercise

When disaster strikes, people have a tendency to give up their usual exercise. Regular, healthy exercise is vital, not only to keep physically fit, but also to help in lowering depression. Especially after a disaster, when the human tendency is to feel depressed, individuals need to maintain a regular schedule for exercise.

Play

Adults play to relax and for enjoyment. For children, however, play has a more important role; it helps them to express themselves. With all the seriousness and depression surrounding a disaster, play is often crucial for children to communicate and vent their feelings. It also serves an important role for parents: by watching children play, they can often discover what is bothering them. Parents can also play with their children, to reassure and comfort them, and get some exercise in the process.

Maintain Routines

The benefits of getting back into old routines quickly has already been discussed. Children need routine. It orders their lives, just as it does for adults. Daily routines make people's lives easier, both before and after a crisis.

Keep Rituals

In most societies, rituals mark beginning or endings—the birth of a child, graduation, marriage, the burial of loved ones. Rituals provide meaning and comfort to people's lives. Parents should be aware that for children, it is not only the physical activity of a ritual that is important, but being part of and participating in a meaningful family activity.

7
True Stories: The Blowing Wind

The Wilson family lived near Fort Lauderdale, Florida, slightly inland. Marge and Henry had recently purchased a house and were still in the stage of decorating and furnishing several rooms. Their children Mark, age six, and Helen, age four, attended the local elementary school.

The entire family enjoyed fishing, and had a small boat they parked on a boat carrier by the side of the house. Neither Marge nor Henry were familiar with hurricanes, so they talked to neighbors about what to expect and how to prepare. They purchased flood insurance and stored a box of emergency supplies at the highest level of their home. The house came equipped with pre-cut storm shutters to protect the windows and sliding glass doors, and metal braces to keep the garage door closed. They kept the trees in the yard free of loose and dead branches, in case of powerful winds. Neighbors had also alerted them to the location of evacuation routes. Mark and Helen were too young to take part in much of the preparation, but looked on as their parents got ready.

It was from the six o'clock news that the Wilsons learned of a possible hurricane heading their way. The National Weather

Center measures hurricanes on the Simpson Scale. Categories range from Category One hurricanes, with winds from 74 to 95 miles per hour, to Category Five, marked by winds in excess of 155 miles per hour, catastrophic damage, and waves of eighteen feet or higher. This hurricane was due in twenty-four to thirty-six hours. Still being somewhat unfamiliar with the area, Marge and Henry were not entirely sure whether their house would be in the hurricane's path, but decided to be prepared just in case. They checked their emergency supplies and brought in everything outside that was unsecured, including toys and the lawn furniture. They put on their storm shutters and secured the garage. They moored the boat with chains.

Once the preparations were completed, it was time for the children to go to bed. To prepare them for anything unusual that might happen, Marge and Henry warned them that they may be awakened during the night to go to their grandparents' home. By eleven that night, the hurricane watch had turned into a warning, which meant it would hit within twenty-four hours and have a strength of Category One or higher. There was no order to evacuate, so neither Marge nor Henry were overly concerned. Although anxious, they both tried not to show it to the other. They could hear the wind blowing. Occasionally something would bang against the house. Henry decided to stay awake to see if further information came over the radio or television.

At four in the morning, the order came to evacuate. Powerful wave surges and flooding were becoming a problem, especially along the highways. Henry woke Marge and told her the situation. She dressed the children in warm clothing while Henry loaded the car with emergency supplies. They had already made sure the gas tank was full. Within a very short time they were ready to go. Getting in the car was difficult. High winds necessitated leaning into the wind. Once the supplies were loaded, Henry helped the children to the car. Marge turned off the gas and electricity in the house, and the family left. They were fortunate that the inland roads were not yet flooded, but the roads were crowded. Progress was slow, but they arrived at Henry's parents' house without incident.

The Wilsons waited and watched the progress of the hurricane on television. Powerful surges had inundated several areas, crushing houses, uprooting trees, and tearing roofs off many houses. It wasn't clear whether the wind or the water was doing more damage at this point, at least from watching the continual coverage on television. Finally, the evacuation order was lifted. It was safe to return. The family packed up and headed home. Once again, the trip back was slow, as many families returned to their homes. It was not a happy homecoming.

Henry's boat was destroyed, crushed by tons of water and pulled from its mooring. One corner of the roof had been torn off, allowing water into the house. One of the storm windows must not have been securely fastened, because it too was gone. The house was still standing, but in complete disarray. It would need repair, but could again become livable. Marge and Henry entered the house cautiously, keeping the children behind them. They looked for any animals that might have taken refuge in the house. They opened the windows and doors for ventilation, and to begin the process of drying out the house. When they inspected the utilities, the electricity was functioning properly, but they could not turn on the gas. They would have to call the gas company to do it for them.

For some reason, not all of the rooms were wet. The children's rooms were spared, as was the kitchen. Needless to say, the amount of work needed to get the house back in shape seemed overwhelming. They knew that insurance would pay for the roof and some of the damage, but the task of cleanup alone seemed daunting. The children were excited by the event. They almost seemed to be enjoying themselves. They looked around in awe at the changes to their home. Uprooted trees, damaged buildings, water everywhere—it all seemed strange, yet exhilarating, to them. They quickly ran to neighbors' homes, looking for their friends.

The Wilsons knew that, even with their insurance, this would be an expensive event for them. That and the amount of work to restore their home to its previous condition seemed an enormous burden. They talked of leaving the area, but decided the benefits outweighed the burden. They were going to stay and rebuild.

8

What to Do after a Disaster

Evaluating Your Materials

While no one wishes for a disaster, it is often an invaluable motivation to prepare for another occurrence. This is not as farfetched as it may seem, since aftershocks typically follow earthquakes, hurricanes can turn around and return to their initial place of impact, and in many instances many disasters occur simultaneously—fire, for example, can occur when an earthquake or tornado hits. After a disaster strikes, it is critical to take the time to reexamine materials, the family's needs, and the degree of preparedness for another disaster. If possible, take the time to talk to others to see what their needs were and how they performed. Conversation with others broadens and deepens one's own knowledge and understanding of what to do in an emergency.

In this evaluation, answer the following questions

1. Was the disaster mild or severe?
2. If mild, will additional supplies be needed?

3. When did help arrive? What, if any, was the delay?
4. How was the weather?
5. Where was the closest shelter? Were there others available, and accessible?
6. Was food or water needed?
7. Was there danger of fire, or falling debris?
8. Were clothes or blankets needed?
9. Were communication or signaling devices necessary?
10. What type of transportation, if any, was required? Auto, boat, all-terrain-vehicle?
11. Were fire extinguishers, lights, or candles needed?
12. Did anyone need medical supplies, or first aid?
13. Were important documents kept safe?
14. Were special items needed for babies, the elderly, or the handicapped?
15. What items were most missed?

Once these questions have been answered, restock supplies as soon as possible. Evaluating the first plan and revising it, if necessary, will not only better prepare the family for the next disaster, but will also decrease some of the anxiety left over from the first.

Communication

By nature, disasters tend to isolate people. Communication lines go down and often roads are blocked. We may be able to contact our neighbors unless we live in a more rural area. But most often for the first few hours and sometimes days we may not be able to reach our family members, friends, or important services.

The media can be extremely helpful during disasters. In large-scale disasters that affect an entire area, television and radio news always provide valuable information about where to obtain basic necessities such as food, water, and shelter.

Sometimes evacuation is necessary. This can be traumatic for any family member, but especially for children. Leaving one's home and moving into a large gymnasium with other people of different cultures and socioeconomic levels does not always make for a particularly pleasant change. Although necessary, communicating with Red Cross workers, or people who speak different languages, can be frightening for children initially. But they are often more adaptable than parents and find communication with other children relatively easy.

Some neighborhoods have informal plans and organizations to help one another. This type of communication and involvement is extremely important, since help from local emergency or disaster teams may be slow in coming.

Soon after a disaster is over, renewing social contacts and communication with extended family is an important beginning to the healing process. It is part of getting back into a routine. Plus, friends and family members may either need assistance or be able to provide assistance, both of which can be helpful to the family. Communication and interaction with others provides a healthy emotional outlet, healthier than staying isolated at home or worrying about damage.

Determining Whether You Need Professional Help

As people grow they learn to handle life's problems. But disasters present new, more severe problems that can be overwhelming. Given time, most people eventually work through problems, usually by talking to other people. At times, however, especially with children, the emotional effects of a disaster do not go away. When left alone, they can interfere with school work, social life, sleep, or interpersonal relationships. Within two months, parents will know whether or not their children, or even a spouse, is healing emotionally from the trauma. If it becomes apparent that recovery is not taking place, or seems slow in its progress, professional help should be sought.

As with finding any family doctor or dentist, selecting a psychiatrist to entrust with one's children should be handled with care and caution. Consult pediatricians, personal physicians, school principals, and friends and family for their recommendations. In the absence of those alternatives, consult professional societies, such as local psychological or psychiatric associations to find someone who specializes in working with children. Make sure the initial connection between therapist and child is good. Within a few months, the child should exhibit obvious changes in behavior or progress in recovery. As a parent, be sure you understand what is happening to your child. If you see and can understand the progress, your child is probably in good hands.

Summary

Mentally

1. It is important to find a positive reason for having survived. Whether it is God's will—a message to change one's life, reward for good behavior, a call to be closer to others—or just plain, good luck, the reason makes no difference, as long as it promotes positive feelings and thoughts about being alive.

2. Remembering and forgetting—both are innate defenses that enable the human body to survive trauma. To promote positive feelings, however, it may be valuable to remember events or actions that were courageous, intelligent, helpful, successful, funny, or even lucky. Mistakes or failures can, and should be acknowledged, of course, but only for a brief time, and to learn how to do it differently the next time. Dwelling on negative thoughts or events will slow, and may even stifle, the healing process. Individuals who had low self-esteem or unrealistic expectations of themselves before a disaster may remember only their mistakes, forgetting anything they might have done well. They and people experiencing survival guilt need to reorient their thinking.

3. Developing realistic expectations is crucial, especially for children. Much of children's thinking takes place in the imagination. The younger the child, the more magical his or her thoughts. Think of preparing for disaster like learning to write, or to ride a bike. Both take a tremendous amount of practice. Now compare that to the amount of practice people have handling a crisis, and it becomes apparent that most are vastly underprepared. What's more,

even if someone handles one disaster well, there is no guarantee for a repeat performance.

4. Avoid judgment and criticism. It has a demoralizing effect and increases both anxiety and depression.

5. Focus on the future, rather than rehash the past. This helps to reestablish old routines and supports the healing process.

Emotionally

1. Once physical safety has been established, it is important to acknowledge, allow, and release all feelings. Anger, fear, sadness, guilt, love, gratitude, happiness—whatever their form, feelings should be expressed. They are usually temporary and will change as the healing process begins.

2. Talking is the primary way people express their feelings. With younger children, however, story telling, drawing, and other sorts of play may be more effective. Create an atmosphere of acceptance and warmth, and encourage them to express themselves.

3. Touching, holding, and being physically close to one another are effective, nonverbal ways of communicating support, love, and protection to loved ones.

4. Anticipate emotional mood swings, particularly with feelings of fear or grief. In the first few days or weeks after a traumatic event, expect a roller coaster of feelings. One minute may be marked by euphoria at being alive, while the next may bring feelings of guilt or sadness about surviving, particularly if the disaster took the life of a loved one. Initially, these waves of feeling are intense and come at close intervals, but within two to three months after the event, the intensity lessens and the time between episodes increases. It may take a longer period of time for them to disappear altogether.

5. Time is an important ally in the healing of emotional pain. When people are allowed to express feelings as they occur, the healing process moves more quickly. If the pain is severe or the expression of feelings blocked, however, recovery is much slower.

Physically

1. Rest is necessary after any traumatic event. High levels of stress have accumulated. Individuals may be in new surroundings and around unfamiliar people. There may be physical injuries, painful losses, or intense levels of fear that disrupt sleep. Take time to sleep, or at least rest. An overstressed body can disrupt emotional and mental—as well as physical—functioning.

2. Exercise can reduce excess tension and depression, and aid in the return to normal eating and sleeping patterns. It can also provide an opportunity to get back into a healthy routine. Be sure the exercise is moderate, though; too much exercise can exhaust the body and actually reinforce depression.

3. Play is highly recommended, for both children and adults. Play is different from exercise. Through play, especially nondirected play, people act out mental images in a safe and protected manner. Play opens up the mind to allow thoughts and feelings to come forward. In directed play, parents can make up games with their children, letting them create the rules and characters, assign the roles, and direct the action. Even structured games such as board games can help children release feelings, and can also lead to discussions.

4. Finding meaningful activities for all members of the family is extremely useful in the recovery process. Assigning duties in the cleanup or restoration phase following a disaster will communicate each family member's importance, as well as create a sense of control after what was probably a very out-of-control event.

5. Getting back into a routine as quickly as possible is a good way to reestablish security. If someone is clearly not ready, however, he or she should be given more time and more support.

6. Rituals are important for starting, ending, and transforming experiences. Rituals help people relate to events that go beyond human understanding or control. They provide acknowledgment to a turning point in one's life, marking a beginning or an end. They can also aid in putting a par-

ticular experience in perspective, so that family members can get on with their lives. Burying a loved one—say, a member of the family or a family pet—or creating a ceremony to say good-bye to a home or treasured possessions can launch the process of rebuilding, and help to unify people after a disaster.

Materials

1. Review which materials were actually used during the disaster. Listen to and evaluate what others found useful. A good review will greatly improve preparation for the next disaster.
2. Restock supplies. Add those materials that were needed but missing, and leave out those that were unnecessary.

Communication

1. Reestablish ties with family members, relatives, or friends as time and energy permit. Be prepared for people to ask the same questions over and over. If ease and comfort is gained through retelling, continue. But if the process is irritating or upsetting, tell them that talking about it upsetting and that it may be possible at a later date.
2. If others seem to be moving on more quickly, consider finding a support group, or other outside help, such as making contact with other survivors. Remember, people differ in their need for support and the amount of time it takes to heal.

Environment

1. Take the time to review the larger environmental picture. Determine what, if any, changes need to take place, say, on the house, property, or adjacent property. Political and financial support may be required to make bigger changes. Ascertain what other escape routes, shelters, high or low areas, and so on, may be available. If the chance of a reoccurrence is too terrifying, however, and that chance is likely, consider moving.

Determining Whether You Need
Professional Help

Forty-five to sixty days is usually sufficient time to determine whether or not someone is recovering, except, of course, in the cases of paralysis, amputation, or other injuries that require extended medical treatment. Many people start the process of rebuilding their lives sooner. While that process may not be complete—for example, it may take a long time to get money from insurance or federal emergency assistance agencies—it is in progress. People have gone back to work and started rebuilding their homes. They may not be feeling great, but they are at least functioning. If someone is still traumatized after sixty days, seek professional help as soon as possible.

Activities to Help Children Express Their Feelings after a Disaster

Just as professionals use defusing and debriefing techniques to help people get in touch with feelings, parents can use various techniques to help their children talk and express their feelings. Several are outlined below. The relationship between all of these methods is fuzzy. They all blend together in some areas. Some methods will work with one child, while others will work for another. For example, some children may use toys such as puppets or toy houses to tell their story, while others may be able to express themselves verbally.

These approaches are useful because often children are unable to tell parents how they feel, either because they do not want to, or their feelings are unconscious and therefore not available to them. Children need to be taught diverse ways to deal with their reactions to stress, and given practice so they can use them as needed. Parents should use those approaches most comfortable to them, and to their children. Whatever the method, take care when exploring children's feelings. Parents need to validate—not criticize—these feelings, whatever they are. They need to tell their children that their feelings are normal and expected, given the circumstances, and that they are not crazy or weird. Only when children feel free to open up and express themselves will they do so.

Timing is also very important. Parents must respect their children's wishes if they are not ready to talk. Some children have great difficulty opening up and discussing their feelings directly. If this is so, use other methods to allow them to express feelings. Some children are more willing to express their feelings—especially feelings of guilt and fear—if their parents admit having these same feelings; it creates the freedom and safety for children to reciprocate. Much of a child's willingness and comfort with expressing feelings depends on his or her predisaster experiences and personality. If the child is not used to sharing feelings with the family, it is unlikely it will happen after a disaster. Some families teach their children to keep feelings to themselves. Parents might give some thought as to what they are teaching their children, and consider what effect it might have in a disaster.

Family Members

Initially, children derive their self-esteem from their parents. Children who are supported emotionally are better able to adjust both in and after stressful situations. To begin, hold a family meeting, if appropriate. Encourage everyone to share their feelings. If parents and older siblings participate, younger children will likely follow. If such a meeting would not be appropriate, given certain family dynamics or special circumstances, the parent with whom the child feels most comfortable should arrange a time to talk privately with the child. Or, see if the child will feel comfortable discussing feelings with a close relative. During any discussions of feelings, it is crucial that the child feel safe. The following techniques create an atmosphere of safety and acceptance.

Listen; allow the child to talk.

Focus on the child's problem.

Accept and acknowledge the child's feelings, whatever they are.

Be patient.

Do not make promises that are impossible to keep.

Do not blame.

Friends

Whom do children confide in and talk to most often? Their
friends. Research shows that children are more likely to discuss
their feelings with a group of their peers, whom they know and
usually play with, than with parents or other adults. Sometimes
getting a group of friends together, giving them play materials,
and then listening quietly will bring about the desired results.
Consider inviting neighborhood or other close friends and listening to them while they play, or talking to them as a group. The
results can be dramatic. Questions or topics that might be helpful
are listed in the next section. Remember, there are no right or
wrong questions, only questions that are successful or unsuccess-
ful in getting children to talk. It's important to remember, too,
that oftentimes other children will try to answer a question asked
of another child. Allow this to occur. Peer relationships help
reduce feelings of isolation and allow children to see how other
children deal with problems.

The Talking Approach

This approach can be used in a private conversation with a child,
or a group discussion with the whole family or friends. The conversation might flow naturally, or asking questions may be necessary to keep the conversation going if it begins to lag. Some possible questions are listed below. Tailor them to the occasion, and to
the children's needs. Whatever the questions used, children
should not be forced to answer. They should also be free to ask
their own questions if they want to. The more children trust the
adult present, the freer they feel, and the more apt to answer they
are.

What happened?
What did you see?
What did you hear?
What did you smell?
How do you feel now?
What were you doing during the disaster?
What was your first thought?
What were you thinking while it was going on?
How did you feel when it began?

What did you do when it started?

What did you want to do after it started?

What did other people around you do?

Was anything broken during the disaster?

Were you hurt at anytime?

Was anybody else hurt?

Were any of your pets hurt or scared?

Do you feel sorry for anything you did, or didn't do?

Have you been able to sleep since it happened?

Have you had any bad dreams?

Do you keep thinking about it?

What is different since the disaster happened?

What do you do to make yourself feel better?

What's the worst thing that happened?

What would you do differently now that you know what happened?

It's important that the answers to these and other questions be voluntary. Children should not feel compelled to answer, or to explain the answer, if they don't want to. It's also important to know that it's all right to directly ask children how they feel. They may or may not answer. But it's important to ask, nonetheless. After a disaster, many children have reported not wanting to worry their parents by expressing their own scary feelings, but have said they would have discussed them had their parents asked directly.

Another verbal way to get children to express themselves is to use stories. Stories have been used for centuries to convey history, moods, and different behaviors. Children have a natural affinity to stories, especially those in which puppets, photos, and drawings are used for illustration. Some children may have difficulty making up their own story. In this case, telling a story about a same-sex, same-age child going through the same type of disaster may stimulate the child to join in.

The Drawing Approach

The drawing approach encourages self-expression through a combination of drawing and talking. Offer children a box of colored crayons and suggest they draw anything of interest that happened before, during, or after the incident. Their drawing will reveal how they see and feel about the incident, especially what was important and not important to them. In the absence of pressure or cues from adults, children will draw something that expresses their own interest, feelings, or thoughts. The quality of the drawing is not important; even a stick figure will do. What is important is that parents see what their children draw and hear what they say about the drawing. That combination will enable parents to understand what is most important to, and what most affected, their children. If some children do not want to draw a picture, draw one for them, and then discuss some possible interpretations.

The drawing approach accesses children's fantasies, as well as their ability to communicate feelings and ideas. If these feelings are guarded, the process can be frustrating and disappointing for parents. But remember, whatever comes out of these sessions is important. It is what the child is able to talk about at that moment. Parents may also need their child to interpret the picture for them. A series of black lines may seem like insignificant scribbles to a parent, but may mean a great deal to the child. Some children may draw several pictures and discard them. This does not matter; it reflects underlying conflicts. The goal is to get the child to talk about what is important to him or her. It provides an outlet for feelings, and the expression of those feelings, which is an excellent way to reduce stress. Children benefit from expressing feelings in a safe environment, just as adults do.

Art therapy constitutes an entire field of rehabilitation in which both children and adults are encouraged to express themselves with paints and crayons. Although parents are not therapists, they can use this approach to allow their children to tell their story.

The Play Approach

Everything people do is, in some way, an expression of themselves. Dress, language, and other physical presentation are all personal, unique illustrations of personality. It's easy to conclude that the man who likes to play football differs from the man who likes to play chess. The nice thing about play is that people usually choose it themselves and stay with it only as long as it interests them or gives them pleasure. Children also choose games that interest and satisfy them. For example, children who have survived a disaster may make up a game that allows them to relive some of the experience, but in a controlled, careful way. Changes in children's play point to changes they are going through, and those things that are important to them.

Psychologists frequently allow children to pick a game to play during therapy. They use the game both to interpret behavior as well as a vehicle of self-expression. Asking open-ended questions while they're playing a game also frees them to express themselves. Ask questions such as "What is happening?" or "What have you been doing?" or more direct questions like "How did you sleep last night?" or "What did you dream about?" or "What bothers you most now?" Almost any game can be used to help children express themselves. Children enjoy and are accustomed to games, so this type of questioning enables them to talk freely and comfortably. And if they are not ready to talk, children will relay that message very clearly by avoiding the questions, or asking to play something else.

Talking, drawing, game playing, story telling, sharing with family and friends—all happen at different times. What is important is children's readiness to talk and parents' sensitivity to their children.

Other Approaches

There are many other approaches to helping children discuss their feelings. Some work for one child, others work for another. Parents should use approaches that they consider appropriate and effective for their own children. If none of the methods outlined above work, parents should develop their own. For example, one father takes long walks with his son and daughter, talking and sharing along the way. Most children will talk about what is important to them if parents listen and are not critical. Using the television to start a discussion is another option. Constant, continual television coverage of a disaster can sometimes overwhelm children, but it may also help them to understand the event, and may provide an excellent starting point for a conversation.

Keep in mind that children younger than five have much more difficulty with verbal expression, while those ten years or older, particularly young teenagers, will probably be more vocal about their concerns and feelings. If older children talk too much, it is because they need to. The more parents allow them to talk and express their thoughts and feelings, whatever they may be, the better off older children will be. This may be trying for some parents—especially if they disagree with what their children are saying, or if they are dealing with their own problems at the time—but patience is crucial. Children need to know that whatever they feel following a disaster is normal. They need to feel that they are not bad for feeling what they do feel, and that the situation will improve with time.

9
Help after a Disaster

When disaster strikes there is often little or no time to seek help. Many people, by and large, are on their own. Adequate preparation and sensible, effective planning carries most through for a period of time, but it is helpful to know that a whole network of agencies and individuals are organized and trained to help after a disaster.

Which individuals and agencies actually help, and in what order, depends on the extent of the disaster, and location of those needing assistance. The weather and the condition of roads may be some variables. The availability of communication may be another.

What Types of Help Are Available?

Family

In any disaster the family is usually the first line of defense. The immediate family, or, sometimes, the local family, is usually the single most important factor in a child's welfare. Children live by routine. Any change in routine and surroundings may cause anxiety. Often, if parents are not hurt, or overwhelmed by the traumatic event, holding and talking to children goes a long way toward relieving their stress. How parents act will determine the level of stress or fear their child senses in the immediate environment. If parents are unable to render assistance to their children, a relative with whom the child is familiar and comfortable may be the next best person to help.

Friends and Neighbors

Children may also feel comfortable with friends or neighbors. Construct a mutual agreement with friends and neighbors to provide assistance in the event of a disaster. Plan ahead to stay with them, if necessary, for a short period of time. By making the agreement mutual, there will be no need to feel guilty. What is important is that your children are safe and in a familiar environment.

Local Religious or Volunteer Organizations

Sometimes local religious organizations or volunteer organizations offer help such as a shelter, food and water, blankets and cots, and other emergency medical supplies. Find out in advance which organizations offer this assistance after a disaster. Many national organizations, such as the American Red Cross and Salvation Army, also offer local assistance.

Local Fire and Police Departments

Fire and police departments are often able to provide assistance, or, if occupied with emergencies, may be able to direct people to the appropriate organization for help. In the event of a disaster, these organizations are alerted to which shelters are available and where to go for specific medical or other assistance. Most important, they may be able to provide quick assistance to those trapped, hurt, or in danger.

The American Red Cross

The American Red Cross, which is part of the International Red

Cross, is organized and trained to help communities struck by any natural or human-made disaster. Specifically, the Red Cross may provide, shelter, food, water, sleeping accommodations, medical assistance, and communication assistance to families. Its shelters may be in churches, schools, or other safe buildings that can house a number of people. The Red Cross also provides psychological counseling to individuals and families in a disaster through its mental health disaster team.

City or County Departments of Health and Mental Health

Health and mental health agencies may also offer help, either on their own or through Red Cross shelters. After the 1994 earthquake in Los Angeles, the Los Angeles Department of Mental Health, in conjunction with FEMA, the Federal Emergency Management Agency, formed Project Rebound to help with the psychological aftereffects and other types of assistance regarding property damage. Other cities and counties, large and small, have their own emergency plans to assist in a disaster.

Hospitals and Schools

Most hospitals have plans in place to deal with large-scale emergencies. Most schools across the country have procedures and plans in place for a variety of disasters, depending where they are located. Rehearsals prepare children on what to expect and what to do in the event of a disaster. Sometimes, plans are made to evacuate before a disaster strikes, such as in hurricane country. Again, it is the preparation that is most helpful.

City, State, County, and Federal Emergency or Disaster-Relief Organizations

Literally thousands of organizations are available to help in a disaster, too numerous to mention here. Whether minimal or extensive, every state and city has plans in place to deal with emergencies. If the disaster is on a large enough scale, the federal government may declare its location a national disaster area and allot funds for special assistance.

Business Organizations

Some business organizations provide assistance during a disaster. One example is cellular phone companies, which may donate both the equipment and air time to those in need.

The Collective Conscience

It is heartwarming to learn how generous individuals can be in a crisis. As emergency disaster organizations become better prepared and better trained, help is given more quickly to those in need. In particularly devastating disasters, other countries have even stepped in to assist. What is important to remember is that letting someone know they need assistance is up to the victims themselves. In the turmoil of a disaster, and the confusion that typically follows, it may be difficult to locate help. Use any communication necessary to obtain it.

When Should You Seek Professional Help?

Often psychological problems are resolved in a short period of time after a disaster occurs. But when problems persist, parents need to be aware that professional help may be necessary to resolve the trauma some family members cannot overcome. Sometimes, seeking this help sooner, rather than later, is wise.

Psychiatrists, psychologists, marriage and family counselors, social workers, psychiatric nurses, and other mental health workers are all available to help children work through the feelings that occur during a disaster. Some specialists are trained specifically to help disaster survivors, such as those in the American Red Cross, emergency and disaster agencies, and in state and city departments of mental health.

In the last few years a number of individuals around the country have become specialists in the study of disasters. Dr. George S. Everly Jr. and Dr. Jeffrey M. Lating co-authored a recent book called *Psychotraumatology: Discussing the Results of Disasters Such As Posttraumatic Stress*. Dr. Jeffery Mitchell, in 1989, founded the International Critical Incident Stress

Foundation, and with Dr. Everly, has written numerous books and papers on how to help individuals after a disaster. These books outline the steps to helping individuals and groups through such methods as immunization, one-on-one intervention, debriefing, and other support programs. Dr. Mitchell's critical incident stress debriefing is one of the best known and most widely used methods of preventing or mitigating posttraumatic stress. Many disaster workers have taken Dr. Mitchell's seminars and are trained in helping individuals after a disaster. Business organizations are also using these methods to help employees to overcome disaster trauma so they can resume normal functioning and performance.

Of most use to parents is Mitchell and Everly's finding that early professional help can be enormously helpful in getting family members back to normal functioning. Rather than a parent or child being psychologically disabled for months, or even years, early mediation can resolve potential difficulties in a matter of hours.

If, after a disaster, a loved one appears to be suffering from severe stress or appears to be in shock, and the symptoms do not lessen or go away with time, seek professional help. Call the family physician, local psychological association, or local office of the American Red Cross for some names of professionals trained to deal with disaster trauma.

10

True Stories: The Burning Forest

Marge Woosterman lived with her son, David, in a rustic, two-story house on the edge of a national forest in Oregon. After her husband died, she had decided to move to a place where she had always wanted to live. At thirty-eight, what she felt she wanted was solitude, to pursue her painting. David, who was twelve years old, attended a private school, close enough that he could walk home. She felt she had all she needed: beautiful scenery, a change of seasons, two beloved cats, her son, and the lifestyle she craved. She had chosen her house, which sat halfway up the mountain, for the marvelous view and the sunlight that lit her studio. She cherished the greenness and freshness of the landscape, and considered its frequent rain a small price to pay for its beauty.

Every several years, the rains were followed by drought, which frequently led to fires. But there was a system in place that warned of fire, so she knew when it was time to leave, should evacuation be necessary.

Fire is a natural process. Forest fires have been around as long as fire itself. They can be extremely destructive, and dangerous to humans, if they get out of control. September and October were usually hot and dry in Oregon; most of the fires occurred during those months. This particular October followed a typical wet season. The adjacent forest was filled with dead branches, and dried, fallen leaves covered its floor. David made his usual forays into the forest, marking his trail Indian style, he felt, so that he wouldn't get lost. On this particular day in October, he was walking through the woods when he began to smell burning wood. It was an unmistakable smell; he had learned about forest fires in school. He began to run toward home.

How the fire started was never deciphered. Forest fires are frequently started by careless hikers, but not always. David could not see any flames, but the smell was growing stronger. When he looked up he could see the smoke. As he neared home he could hear his mother calling him frantically. Relief covered her face when she saw him.

Marge had the television on, listening and waiting to see whether this was a small fire that would burn itself out or a massive conflagration that would spread through the forest quickly, threatening homes on its edge. Its size was medium, the news reported, but it was uncontrolled. To be safe, Marge began to fill her car with essential supplies: personal papers, special medicines, a few of her paintings, and some clothes. Since the fire was not yet threatening, she felt she was being overly cautious, but preparing made her feel safer. David was now safe; he was home, watching television. Her cats were also indoors, although they tended to come and go as they pleased.

Several hours later it became clear that this fire was a threat. A powerful wind system, with hot wind gusts and fire whirls, was moving the blaze steadily through the forest. And a steady wind was blowing in the direction of the highway, and in the direction of Marge's house. Although her house was only halfway up the mountain, Marge knew that fire has a natural tendency to rise. She didn't want to be caught surrounded by fire and unable to reach the highway. As she watched the news closely, trying to decide what to do, the local forest ranger drove up in a truck. He suggested that she move out within the next thirty minutes. All indications were of continued wind, with a possibly serious threat of fire and damage for the residents in her area.

Marge asked David to get the cats and put them in the car. Unfortunately, one of the cats was nowhere to be found. By this time they could not only smell the smoke but began to feel the heat of the fire. With heavy hearts, they left the cat behind and evacuated the area. The question was where to go. Marge had not yet made many friends in the area. Nor did she have any relatives to go to. At the bottom of the mountain, she was stopped by a police car who mentioned a Red Cross shelter at the local high school. Marge knew the way. It was in a safe area away from the fire.

This was Marge's first experience in a shelter. It did not look particularly inviting at first glance. Cots were lined up, row after row, equipped with a blanket, pillow, and very little space on either side. She and David were received pleasantly, however, and were assigned adjacent cots. Marge was told where to find food and water, and was given several extra blankets. She also learned there was medical care available as well. David immediately met some friends and went off to play with them. Food and water was plentiful. These were not gourmet meals, but nobody complained. Marge met some neighbors whom she had seen before at the local store and post office. She had brought food for her cat, which was confined to a cage unless taken out on a leash to walk around. As she placed some food and water in the cat's cage, Marge again began to worry about her other cat.

There was one large television in the center of the back wall, for people to check the progress of the fire. Almost everyone in the room focused the screen, watching the path of the blaze. Several people sobbed as they watched it threaten the highway, and then their homes. Volunteer counselors from the Red Cross and the local health department approached those individuals most visibly disturbed and offered their assistance. There were few private rooms, but there was space set aside for that purpose.

After two days Marge and David were able to sleep more easily. Other people's noise did not bother them as much. Waiting to take a shower was annoying, but everyone seemed willing to wait; after all, they had no choice. Information over the news suggested that the fire was starting to die down. That afternoon, an announcement was made at the shelter that everyone was allowed to return home. The shelter would stay open for those whose homes had burned. Not knowing what had happened to their home left both Marge and David quite anxious, but they headed home, eager to get back to normal living. On the drive back, each thought about their home, the lost cat, and their favorite possessions, hoping they would find them intact. For people who like solitary living, a shelter can be a trying experience, with people of many cultures and mixed languages living closely together. David had a good time, all in all, but Marge was eager to get home.

As they drove up the mountain, they could see the devastation. Some homes escaped the blaze untouched. Some, however, were completely burned to the ground, with only brick chimneys left standing. As they drove farther up the mountain the smell intensified, as did their anxiety. As they neared the edge of their property, they saw the house. It was still standing, but the damage was evident. The deck facing the forest was still there, but severely charred. A familiar face greeted them as Marge drove up the driveway. There was the cat, unhurt, but hungry, thirsty, and meowing mightily. David scooped him up in his hands. Marge threw her arms around both of them and started to cry. They had been lucky; they were together and they were safe.

11
Special Family Problems after a Disaster

Certain problems may occur with some family members as the process of staying together and trying to heal unfolds. Specifically, these problems may occur with the following:

the elderly
a spouse
a child
an adolescent
a member of the family who is disabled in some way, such as
    blind or deaf, in a wheelchair, or in some way handi-
    capped
someone hurt in a disaster

Ways to help each of these groups are outlined separately below.

Helping the Elderly after a Disaster

Although it is normal for everyone to feel vulnerable after a disaster, the elderly feel a more severe loss of control over their own lives. Physical limitations, in particular, tend to make the elderly feel especially vulnerable in disasters. Because the elderly often feel isolated from the world, any disruption in their routine raises special anxieties. These anxieties and fears give rise to both emotional and physical symptoms. It is sometimes difficult in an emergency to understand how important these symptoms are.

Typical emotional reactions of the elderly include

fear of being hurt physically
fear of being alone
fear of being abandoned
forgetfulness
irritability and quick anger
disorientation and confusion
sadness and depression
difficulty sleeping

Typical physical reactions include

difficulty breathing
exaggeration of any pre-incident physical problem(s)
headaches
aches and pains
sleep disorders
vomiting
bowel and urinary problems
lethargy

It is usually better for elderly people to remain with their family, rather than be separated, particularly if they appear disoriented. Staying with the family helps them to orient themselves to what is going on. As the family talks openly about their feelings it will help the elderly to do the same. Touching them can be reassuring. Giving them a useful task can also be helpful, if they can handle it, such as caring for one of the children, or helping prepare food. Just as it is helpful for the rest of the family to work together, it is helpful to the elderly to see themselves as a needed and useful part of the family.

Helping a Spouse after a Disaster

People's reactions to disaster can vary widely. Sometimes a spouse can be particularly disturbed after a disaster. What is important to do, for whoever is upset, is to help resolve the problem as quickly as possible. Holding and reassuring a spouse can be helpful. Assigning him or her a useful task is life affirming, and reinforces the role of parent. Holding the family together and returning to as normal a routine as the situation allows is extremely important. Talking about feelings of fear and anxiety is healthy. Even when the repetition grows tiresome, it is important to allow individuals to talk as much as possible about the incident. Talking it out, or catharsis, helps people overcome feelings of confusion and anxiety more quickly. All of the techniques above are helpful. The technique of using denial is not. That is, telling a spouse that it was no big deal, or that the danger is over, is not particularly reassuring.

If nothing works and it becomes clear that professional help is needed, do not delay. The quicker a spouse receives help, the sooner the problem will be solved.

Helping the Truly Upset Child after a Disaster

Although all family members are affected by a disaster, sometimes it is one child who seems to need more help than the others. This child may cry more, or cling more tightly to parents. For young children, holding and reassuring them is a good first step. Talking about their feelings is an excellent way for older children to deal with their feelings. For the child who is silent and lethargic, parents need to prompt a discussion. It may be helpful for parents to share their feelings, such as "I was scared when it happened, weren't you?" Again, allowing the child to help in what is seen as a useful way is often an important part of, and first step in, recovering from a disaster. When a child sees that he or she has a role in the family, and can help constructively, he or she recovers much more quickly. Returning to the normal routine, including playing with friends, also helps a traumatized child recover.

Helping an Adolescent after a Disaster

Adolescents have a difficult time adjusting to disasters. They are neither children nor adults. They are trying to be more adult, yet may regress to earlier, more childish behavior. After a disaster adolescents often become irritable and easily angered, without knowing why. They need to verbalize these feelings and admit to feeling fear and anxiety. As they understand that their reactions are normal, even for adults, they begin to improve. Their postdisaster behavior needs to be watched to make sure they are not just denying feelings, but handling them constructively. As with all family members, adolescents benefit by being some responsibility to help out. These should be more adult responsibilities in the family, if they are able to handle them.

Helping the Handicapped after a Disaster

The handicapped, like the elderly, live with a sense of vulnerability at all times. If, for example, someone is in a wheelchair and an earthquake or a fire strikes, that person is especially vulnerable. Electricity may be shut off, rendering elevators inoperable. If phone lines are down, there may be no way to get help. Even if handicapped individuals survive, at best, their routine is disrupted. Expect them to be especially fearful and anxious. They may show a good deal of anger, not only at family members, but at themselves and the world around them. They will need special care, possibly for a short period of time, until they are in what they consider a safe situation.

Helping the Injured after a Disaster

Aside from being hurt physically, there is little as painful as a loved one being hurt. Immediately following a disaster, check on everyone in the family. Then, return to those who are hurt and make some quick decisions: Do they need emergency help, such as stopping the flow of blood? Should they be moved? Can they be moved? Those with possible back or neck injuries should be moved only if it is necessary to save their lives. Call for medical help immediately. If phone lines are down, find someone who knows basic first aid. It may be wise to invest the time in taking such a course, before disaster strikes. Keep them warm. If the roads are clear, take them to the nearest emergency room. Be sure to know where the nearest emergency facility is.

If someone is stuck in a building, or trapped under heavy debris, one person should call for help while the other stays with the person trapped. The person calling for help should be prepared to provide directions, if rescuers require it.

12

Cultural Differences in Handling Stress and Disasters

Not only do people handle stressful situations differently, based on personality, experience, and training, there are also vast differences in the way different cultures handle stress. In some cities—Los Angeles, New York, and Chicago, to name a few—more than forty different languages are spoken. This becomes a problem when people are offered help that they don't want, or do not receive help in a way they can accept. Although professional disaster workers are trained to be aware of cultural differences, they are often not trained well enough to deal with many diverse cultures. For example, the routine practice of trying to find someone nearby who speaks discernable English is not always an option in some communities. Or, directions being given by a child who is translating is not acceptable to people of some cultures. Whatever the circumstance, remember that those who provide help may come from a different cultural background and do not intend to be rude or unhelpful; rather, there is likely a communication problem. In smaller towns the likelihood of such problems is reduced, although not impossible.

Parents should also be aware of their own subculture, and how it may or may not differ from the larger culture in which they live, so they are not offended by professionals and/or volunteers who come to their aid.

Different cultures look at various aspects of life differently. How pain is handled is one example. Some cultures are more stoic than Americans and deal with pain differently. They may also handle feelings of grief differently. What embarrasses one group may not embarrass another. Respect should be cultivated, for differences as well as similarities, by both sides. In large disasters, help may come from all over the country, or even different countries. Be prepared to accept help from whomever offers it, in whatever form it is offered.

How to Communicate with Disaster Workers from Other Cultures

These problems may never arise. In an ideal situation, every emergency worker would know the language and customs of every culture he or she encounters. But the world is not ideal, nor are the circumstances in a disaster. Basic communication about shelter, food, and water are usually possible, but more complicated communication may not be. Volunteers are often taught to show respect for all people with whom they work, but it doesn't always work that way.

These types of problems frequently show themselves in shelters. Many different cultural groups are forced to come together, sleep in the same room, eat together, all for the first time. Cultural and personal differences are bound to be abrasive at times and can only be worked out if there is an attempt at mutual respect. Most people would normally shudder at the thought of having to sleep in the same room with a total stranger. But in a disaster, one large room becomes a shelter, housing several hundred strangers. Noises and languages may sound strange. Smells are different. Territorial differences, that is, the area assigned to one family, may arise. Yet, strange as it seems, these problems are often overcome by the goodwill of everyone who is experiencing the same problems. Children especially seem to have little difficulty with the unusual and crowed conditions of a shelter. Whenever possible, most Red Cross shelters attempt to have volunteers on staff who can translate.

Again, the only thing that works in dealing with cultural and language differences is mutual respect—respect by the workers for the families with whom they are in contact, and respect by the families for those who are trying to help.

13
True Stories:
The Crazy Man

September was a warm and lazy month in Eaton, a small mid-western town, home to five thousand. The younger children reluctantly gave up their summer play, as they headed back to Munroe Elementary School, one of two elementary schools in town. Evan Simpson, a local pharmacist, kept busy selling every-thing from candy bars to prescriptions. His wife, Shirley, helped him out when he got busy, but mostly stayed home to care for their children, Evan Jr., age eight, and Gloria, age seven. They were a church-going family, and Shirley also helped out at the church from time to time.

On Tuesday morning, Shirley made breakfast as usual. She called upstairs to the children, urging them to hurry. They weren't late yet, but Shirley was careful that they kept good atten-dance. After she dished up everyone's breakfast, she neatly assembled their lunches—a sandwich, chips, an apple, and a snack dessert for each. Evan dropped off the kids at school on his way to work. Aside from the argument about who was going to sit in front today, the family discussed their upcoming weekend plans. They were going to the city to visit the grandparents. It was an overnight visit, and a trip the children were looking forward to.

Evan's pharmacy was not far from the children's school. It was a quiet neighborhood with little crime, although concern about drug use was on the rise among parents of the older children. One end of town seemed to be a crime magnet, not only for drugs, but for other crimes as well. Although rare, when something bad happened in town, it was usually on the south side. Last year's rape, for example, occurred in the southern portion of town, which also saw several muggings and even one murder. Evan and his family rarely traveled through that area.

It was about eleven o'clock that sunny Tuesday morning when a young husky man with long black hair and a small goatee walked through the school gates carrying a pistol, a Vietnam-era hand grenade, and a recent civilian model of the AK-14 machine gun. The pistol was in its holster, the grenade in his pocket, but he handled the machine gun as if he had used it before. Talking and laughing to himself, he began firing at the children on the playground.

Evan Jr. was hit in the leg and fell to the ground. Other children did not fare as well; some died instantly as they were hit by the first barrage of bullets. The children screamed and began crying. The gunman pointed the gun at the principal who had just emerged from his office and forced him into a second grade classroom. Mr. Egrin, the principal, tried to calm the gunman and find out what he wanted. At first the gunman was incoherent. Finally, when asked if he wanted money, he seemed to pull himself together. Yes, money is what he wanted. Not being particularly knowledgeable about the effects of various drugs, Mr. Egrin did not know what the gunman was on, but was sure he was on something.

The children in the classroom were mixed in their reactions. Not knowing what transpired on the playground, they weren't sure what the man would do. Gloria, who was among those in the classroom, was terrified. She knew about guns. Her father, who liked to hunt and fish when he had time away from the pharmacy, had cautioned her to be very careful of them. She had learned that guns could kill and were not to be played with. Gloria grew more afraid as the gunman waved the gun around the room, sometimes pointing it toward her.

Meanwhile, the school alarm had gone off. Teachers were keeping their classrooms inside to be safe. The secretary had already called the local police and told them of the problem. They, in turn, notified the sheriff for additional reinforcements and immediately headed toward the elementary school. The children on the playground who were not hurt began to run through the school gates to get to safety. Evan Jr. was lifted up and carried away. As the ambulance arrived, he was the first one put inside. The paramedic who was in the ambulance attended to him immediately. Since the gunman seemed content to stay in the second grade classroom, police began clearing out the rest of the school. The school buses were there, so they loaded the children up and sent them home. If parents were not at home the children were taken to a local church to be picked up by their parents.

Parents were being notified, one by one, including Evan at the pharmacy. When he got the call, he immediately closed the store and drove quickly to the school. He knew his daughter was in that classroom. Shirley had gone to the hospital to be with Evan Jr.

Evan was not allowed on the school grounds. There were enough police to keep everyone at a safe distance away from the school. The gunman fired his machine gun up into the air, trying to scare the kids and Mr. Egrin. Fortunately, no one was hurt. He then threw away his gun and drew his pistol in one hand; he held the hand grenade in the other. The police called for him to come out, but he refused, threatening to shoot more children. After ten minutes, the police called for a rifle team. These sharpshooters, part of the sheriff's department, were used when all else failed.

The school windows were large. One man was able to get a good shot and took it. The gunman fell over. He was not dead, but had a serious chest wound. The police rushed in and handcuffed him while others rescued the children. Twenty crying second graders are a handful. When out of danger, the children were turned over to their parents. Evan took Gloria in his arms and held her, trying to hold back his own tears at what might have happened. He took Gloria to the hospital to see his wife and Evan Jr.

Seven children died that day at school. The town was in mourning. The school was closed for the next two days. Children who were not hurt were traumatized. Parents were very upset. The school board met, and called the State Board of Education and the American Red Cross for assistance. Both organizations had counselors. The Red Cross immediately set up a Critical Incident Stress Management Program. Teachers were given a chance to work through their feelings about what happened, and about what might have happened. Parents were also invited to a Critical Incident Stress Debriefing. They talked not only about how upset they were, but how upset their children were.

As many in the city attended the funerals of the seven children, the town began slowly to heal. The local newspaper dubbed it the worst disaster ever to have occurred in the city. All because of "The Crazy Man," as the children called him. The children, especially, needed a great deal of help. School counselors and teachers did debriefing work with them. Evan, Shirley, Evan Jr., and Gloria saw a counselor. Through therapy, Evan and Shirley realized the terror their children felt, and that which they felt themselves. After several weeks, the entire family was moving toward recovery, or so it seemed.

Evan Jr. recovered fairly quickly from his wound, but had a permanent scar on his leg to remind him. Gloria took much longer to recover. She, like many other children, had nightmares for months. She dreamt of "The Crazy Man," waking up terrified and sobbing. Her schoolwork suffered, too. She was unable to concentrate in class, or on anything for any length of time. After several months of therapy, and the support of her family, Gloria eventually made an excellent recovery. The incident was not forgotten; it would be a permanent part of their lives. What was gone was much of the pain and anguish they had felt.

14
An Overview of Some Disasters

Tornadoes

Tornadoes are the most violent of windstorms. Violent whirling winds pull everything in their path inward and upward, leaving a great deal of damage and destruction. Tornadoes are known for destroying everything along their path. While that path is sometimes narrow, it is often difficult to predict its direction. Twisters move from side to side, in a circle, and along a straight line. The use of radar and individual spotters has greatly enhanced warning and tracking technology, but if a tornado springs up suddenly, people may have as little as five minutes to get to safety. Having a radio or television on hand will increase that time.

Thunderstorms can also produce tornadoes, which are essentially enormous concentrations of energy. In the United States, tornadoes appear mostly in the Midwest, particularly Oklahoma, Kansas, Nebraska, and Missouri. People often hear a whistling sound as tornadoes approach, caused by their immense speed, which is sometimes as high as 325 miles per hour. The pressure created by these gigantic vacuums can lift almost anything in their path: cars, roofs, trees, boats, people, and so on.

As in any disaster, planning is the first step. If sufficient warning is provided by radio or television news, leaving to find a safer area is a good option. If not, and the funnel, or spout, is visible, the best option is to seek shelter in the basement of a protected, solid building or, as is often done in the states mentioned above, move into an already prepared storm cellar. Failing that, seek shelter indoors, beneath an interior door frame or other structurally sound portion of the building.

Because damage to houses, particularly roofs, is not unusual in a tornado, it is a good idea to store certain supplies in the basement or storm cellar during tornado season. Tornadoes frequently pass quickly, simply because of their speed, but having emergency supplies on hand, such as food, water, medicine, and a battery-powered radio, may save lives. If new to the area, prepare family members for what to expect. Take a dry run—that is, pretend a tornado is coming and practice the emergency drill. Schools in tornado-prone areas across the country have such drills in place. It would be wise for parents to do the same at home. Contact a local Red Cross office or other disaster agency for other tips on surviving tornadoes.

Volcanoes

Although infrequent, at least on mainland U.S., no other natural event in the world provides such a fantastic view as a volcano. Depending on the amount of energy involved, hot gas combines with other earth materials to form lava which is forced upward, sometimes as powerfully as twenty-five miles per hour. Escaping hot gases and the resultant ash can cross many miles. There are usually warnings that a volcano will soon erupt, but because those warnings are imprecise, they often go unheeded. When Mt. St. Helens erupted a number of families initially refused to evacuate. For some, the decision to move came too late.

Volcanoes can cause other phenomena as well: gigantic rock slides, for example, or floods, if they come in contact with great amounts of snow. The power of the Mt. St. Helens eruption was enormous, the equivalent of twenty-four megatons. The 1815 eruption of Mount Tambora, in Indonesia, was one hundred times more powerful than Mt. St. Helens, with an equivalently greater loss of life. The effects of this and other great volcanoes in history have been felt around the world. The huge amount of ash and smoke produced by Indonesia's Krakatoa, in 1883, deflected enough sunlight that it cooled the earth's temperature by several degrees Fahrenheit. And the amount of dust particles spewn into the atmosphere by the June 1991 eruption of Mount Pinatubo in the Philippines continues to offset the effects of global warming by one degree Fahrenheit each year.

Clearly, there are no halfway measures of escape when threatened by an exploding volcano. Evacuation is necessary, and quickly. This means there is little time to gather necessary supplies. Having an emergency stash essentials, such as required medication, a change of clothes for the family, important documents, water, food, a portable radio, and even camping supplies, if no alternative shelter is available, is crucial. Remember, when the call to evacuate comes, there is no time to gather these items. Preparing an emergency pack beforehand is the only option. That and keeping an adequate supply of gas in the car. Having an emergency pack in the car would be ideal. Just as preparing for a tornado, drills to practice what to do in a volcanic eruption, if appropriate to the area, are a good idea.

Hurricanes

Although not as immediately violent as a tornado, hurricanes can be the most destructive of all storms. Hurricanes are a special type of windstorm that typically strike wide areas and may last for several weeks. Sometimes called typhoons or cyclones, hurricanes cause millions of dollars worth of damage each year and can kill hundreds of people. Hurricanes are caused by the condensation produced when water vapor above the ocean releases heat and meets cooler, drier air. A swirling effect is produced that lasts, on average, nine days and moves approximately twelve miles per hour. The winds, however, can be stronger than two hundred miles per hour, as in Hurricane Janet, in 1955. Huge walls of water, or storm surges, rise up as the hurricane gets closer to land, and crash down powerfully, destroying homes, uprooting trees, flooding roads, and killing people. In fact, nine out of ten people killed in a hurricane are killed by such surges. In 1970, three hundred thousand people died in Bangladesh in a tropical cyclone.

The eastern seaboard of the United States has to deal with hurricanes every year, although most are mild. When they become severe, however, they destroy anything and everything they touch. Thankfully, a sophisticated warning system is in place. The first notice is called a watch, which usually provides twenty-four to thirty-six hours' notice. Hurricane watches are always announced on radio and television, and list available routes to safely travel inland. Having emergency supplies, putting up storm shutters to protect windows and doors, and listening to the media for any changes in a hurricane warning are all essential when a hurricane watch has been announced. Make sure the car has gas and is ready to go, parked away from any trees that might fall on it. Move valuable and personal papers, stored in a waterproof container, to a high spot in the house.

A hurricane notice is upgraded to a warning when it will hit in twenty-four hours or less. Once a warning has been announced, listen to the radio or television for official instructions. If no evacuation order is given, stay inside, away from glass windows and doors. Remember, flooding is a typical effect of hurricanes. Check supplies of water and emergency materials. Make sure a flashlight is handy. Turn off all major appliances to reduce power surges when electricity comes back on.

When the order to evacuate comes, turn off electricity, gas, and water. Pack the car with emergency supplies, including blankets or sleeping bags, and warm clothes. Lock the house and leave. It is often wise to alert a designated person outside the area to the family's destination. Again, practice evacuation drills with the family so each person knows what role to play. Oftentimes there are predetermined shelters set up by the Red Cross. These shelters are always located in a safe area out of the hurricane's path.

Once a hurricane has passed, listen to the radio or television for road conditions and the okay to return home. If necessary, locations of emergency assistance are also reported. Enter the home cautiously, it may be damaged in ways not immediately visible. Check for snakes, insects, or other animals that may have taken refuge from the storm. Contact a professional to turn on utilities. Always keep in mind the extent of damage to the surrounding area. It may be days before grocery stores and other essential services are open and operational. The better prepared beforehand, the easier life is during this difficult time.

As with all major disasters, several agencies, such as the Red Cross, and local, county, state, and federal agencies, will be available to help. How soon this help arrives, however, will depend upon a family's location, the extent of damage, and road conditions. While waiting for help, take precautions such as boiling water in case of contamination.

Floods

Water is essential to human life, and luckily, it is one of the most plentiful substances on earth. Water can be beautiful—people build houses next to it, swim and fish in it, and watch it trickle by. Yet, water can also kill. Floods, usually caused by overflowing banks of rivers, have been known to kill tens of thousands of people. Many countries in the world suffer from floods. The Netherlands are famous for their water-controlling dikes. The United States is famous for its huge dams, as well as the Mississippi levee system used to control rising river water. Dams break, however, as in the infamous Johnstown floods of 1889, and the damage can be overwhelming.

People who live near water need to be prepared for the possibility of flooding. As on the East Coast, areas prone to flooding usually have warning systems in place. When a flood warning comes over the radio or television, the decision must be made whether to evacuate the area or stay and prepare, depending upon the expected severity of the flood. Sometimes, measures can be taken to protect property, such as building dams of sandbags or other material. When the flooding is expected to be severe, however, evacuation is usually the best course of action. Use time wisely. Pack the car with emergency supplies, and make sure it is filled with gas and in good working condition. Listen to the media for which roads are open or closed. Most important, do not wait until the last minute to evacuate. Never underestimate the power of water. In a drinking glass it is inviting; in a flood, it can weigh thousands of tons and move or destroy everything in its way.

Earthquakes

Earthquakes have been in the headlines more often recently, not only because their frequency has increased, but because their severity has increased as well. Earthquakes occur when sufficient strain has built up to cause the earth's rock formations to fracture. Fracture lines are called faults, some of which are known and some of which are unknown. Known faults are frequently active—sometimes very active—while others remain dormant for thousands of years. The Pacific Rim, which includes countries located on or in the Pacific Ocean—such as the western edge of the United States, Canada, Mexico, and South America; the eastern edge of Asia; and Japan—is particularly active. Damage usually ascribed to earthquakes is not always a direct result of the earthquake itself. For example, fires, floods, gas explosions—all are secondary effects of the earth's dramatic movement.

Technology that predicts earthquakes is improving, but is not perfect, and in many cases is imprecise. In earthquake zones many precautionary measures are in place. Special agencies have been created to help in the event of an earthquake. Schools teach children to "duck and cover" during earthquake drills. And many people who live in these areas are well-versed in proper earthquake preparation and reaction. While perfect performance may not always be possible, depending on location, getting away from falling objects and glass is extremely important. More and more buildings in earthquake zones are being built to withstand these quakes, thanks in part to the 1995 earthquake in Kobe, Japan. It seems that each major quake brings with it, aside from catastrophic damage and loss, added improvements and better methods of coping. What parents can do is prepare themselves by having emergency kits at home and in their cars, and listening to radio and television for instructions about how to obtain shelter, food, and first aid, if necessary.

Blizzards and Cold Spells

Blizzards typically occur in the middle interior areas of North America and Eurasia, although they're occasionally found in other parts of the world as well. Blizzards are basically snow storms accompanied by strong winds and low temperatures. It doesn't always have to be snowing, however; powerful winds picking up already fallen snow can create blizzard conditions. In a blizzard, huge snow drifts can trap people, visibility can be reduced to zero, and people can freeze to death. Approximately one-third of all blizzard injuries result from traffic accidents caused by poor visibility, high winds, large snow drifts, and icy roads. The other two-thirds result from overexhaustion or overexposure. Anyone who has tried to make his or her way through a heavy snowstorm, especially when the wind is blowing strongly, knows how much effort it requires. When snow is waist-deep, that effort is tripled. It is easy to be overcome with fatigue when walking through deep snow. And in a blizzard, visibility and movement are hindered further, while snow drifts continue to build faster than it is possible to escape. Skiers, hikers, campers—anyone who is outdoors during a blizzard is in great danger.

Besides the risk of overexhaustion, there is the far greater risk of hypothermia. Hypothermia occurs when the body temperature drops more than four degrees Fahrenheit below normal. The human body cannot withstand this low temperature for any significant length of time. The risk of hypothermia is increased when a person is wet or wearing wet clothes, as is often the case in a snow storm. Even if the temperature is above freezing and there is a sufficient wind chill factor, a person in wet clothes can easily develop hypothermia. It is extremely important to get out of wet clothes as soon as possible. The elderly need special protection in these severe conditions, because their bodies don't produce heat as quickly, and thus, it is much more difficult for them to recover lost body heat.

Blizzards can last from a few hours to several days, depending upon the size and velocity of the storm. But even in a short amount of time roads and power lines can be shut down. During a blizzard, people can easily find themselves without food, electricity, or methods of communication with the outside world.

Therefore, it is necessary for those who live in blizzard-prone areas to have supplies adequate to last several days. Furthermore, no one should ever venture out when warning of a blizzard, or even near blizzard conditions, has been announced, unless it is a life or death situation. As many people found out during the 1977 blizzard that struck Buffalo, New York, becoming trapped in a car is a real possibility.

During that storm, where snow drifted up to four feet in some areas, many people in the downtown area were sent home early as the storm began to worsen. City plows cleared one lane on each road, designating that they be used for emergency and police vehicles only; public and private transportation was forbidden. People already in their cars were trapped by the huge snow drifts that accumulated rapidly. For a twenty-four hour period, visibility was reduced to zero. Many were stranded for days. Food and water had to be shared, and there was a shortage of milk for infants and children. At least nine people died in their cars, from either hypothermia or carbon monoxide poisoning.

If it becomes necessary to wait out a blizzard in a car, use the heater and the engine sparingly and keep a window that is down-wind from the blizzard partially open. Be sure to keep emergency supplies, such as blankets, flares, warm clothing, and candles in the car during blizzard season.

Drought

Drought is defined as an abnormal decline in precipitation which creates severe environmental stress. A drought can begin at any time, last for any number of months or even years, and occur in any climatic region. An extensive drought or one that persists over several seasons can severely undermine an area's resources. Those heavily dependent on their environment are most in danger. As a drought permeates a region vegetation dies, which disrupts both insect and animal life. Over time, drought can transform a once flourishing region into a desert. Areas with extensive drought are subject to dust storms and, on those occasions when it rains, flash flooding.

Starvation, disease, and civil disturbance can all result from extended drought. Insects and animals invade other areas looking for food and water. There may be rationing of resources, such as water for drinking and bathing, as well as waste water for sewers. If severe enough, drought will necessitate permanent evacuation, or result in an enormous change in lifestyle.

Fire

Every year numerous lives are lost to fires. Forest fires, grassland fires, suburban fires, and urban fires can leave devastating destruction and loss of life. Not all fires are bad, however. Some forest fires, for example, are nature's way of replenishing the soil by burning debris on the forest's floor into ash. If not controlled, these fires can endanger others' lives. Fires of this nature are started by lightning, although these represent less than 10 percent of the total number of forest fires. Most are started by human beings, careless campers or hikers and, in the worst cases, arsonists.

Dry, hot, windy weather, especially if prolonged, creates ideal conditions for fire. When exposed to such conditions, wood loses its moisture. In turn, the amount of heat needed to ignite a piece of wood lessens, thereby increasing the danger of fire. In areas at high risk for fire warning signs are posted. During dry weather, many campsites restrict smoking and the use of fire.

Forest fires are often classified into four groups: ground, surface, crown, and mass. Ground fires are usually restricted to thick, dense layers of organic material such as peat deposits. They can smolder underground for months, and usually progress slowly. Extinguishing a ground fire usually requires a large amount of water. When the layer of burning material, or fuel load, is less compact, ground fires can break through the surface to create surface fires.

Surface fires tend to burn material that is above the ground and below tree branches. They tend to move quickly, especially if aided by the wind, consuming primarily grass, bushes, fallen branches, and the chaparral. In most cases, surface fires leave mature trees intact. If the fuel load is high, a surface fire will burn with more intense heat and extend itself into the lower branches of trees, transforming itself into a crown fire.

Crown fires are often less predictable and less controllable than surface or ground fires. If trees are healthy, somewhat separated, and there is little or no wind, crown-grade forest fires usually remain stationary and burn themselves out. If trees are dense, however, the blaze can generate enough heat to create its own wind current and spread itself. The hot air rises, drawing in surrounding air and creating powerful wind vortices that can feed and spread the fire. If there is a ground wind a crown fire can become a running crown fire, which can spread rapidly and reach massive proportions.

Mass fires are large enough and hot enough to create their own wind systems and, depending on the fuel load, weather conditions, and topography, can consume everything in their path.

If ever caught in a forest fire, move away from the fire and, if possible, against the direction of the wind. Wind often dictates the direction a fire will travel. Move into an open, rather than a wooded, area and to lower, rather than higher, ground, since heat naturally rises.

Urban and Suburban Fires

Both urban and suburban areas have distinct fire dangers. Urban areas often have older buildings that may not be up to current fire codes and, in some older cities, may be situated in close proximity of one another. Suburban areas, on the other hand, typically have more fields, parks, open spaces, and trees, providing greater fuel load during dry seasons. Ground winds may be stronger in suburban areas, while vacuum-type winds can be created in urban areas with tall buildings.

In most cases, warning is provided when a fire is moving into the area. But time is critical, often leaving little time for anything other than evacuation. It is always a good idea to keep any important documents in a secure, portable case that can be located and removed quickly. Medication, too, as well as other crucial emergency supplies, should be kept in an accessible, secure place. For those living in areas susceptible to fires, it is a good idea to keep a gym bag with toiletries and a change of clothes in the trunk of the car. Drinking water, a flashlight, important phone numbers, and blankets are also good items to have. In any area, keep a minimum of one-third of a tank of gasoline in the car at all times, just in case of an emergency.

Dealing with Fires

The most critical factor in dealing with any fire is time. The faster some corrective action can take place, the easier the fire will be to put out, whether the fire is in the family home, neighborhood, or outdoors. Swift action can keep a manageable fire from becoming a catastrophe.

Smoke-detector batteries should be checked every six months. Smoke detectors and fire extinguishers should be placed strategically throughout the house. Kitchens, garages, and bedrooms are the areas most often susceptible to fires. Houses with rock or fire-retardant, tile roofs are better protected than houses with shingle or shake roofs.

Neighborhood roads should be wide enough for fire trucks and emergency vehicles to move freely. There should be enough room for fire trucks to turn around. Be sure fire hydrants are free of shrubbery or other landscaping and easily visible. Note which homes have backyard swimming pools that could be accessed in an emergency. In larger fires, where water pressure can decrease because of heavy use, a swimming pool could mean the difference between saving and losing a house.

When camping or hiking, locate firebreaks, lakes, rivers, or streams in the area. Determine whether a fire rescue team could get to the camp location. It only takes a few minutes to imagine how to escape if a fire started in any one of the four directions around you. This simple sixty-second exercise could prevent panic and hasty, unwise action later on. If hiking in an unfamiliar area, be sure to bring along a topographical map and know how to read it. It can show the safest escape route.

Heat Waves

In the city of Chicago during the summer of 1995, more than one hundred people died from exposure to continual, intense heat. Air conditioning units failed; power outages seemed like the norm; and heat rose to record highs, both inside and outside people's homes. Some were able to leave the city, but most were not. Most of the victims were the sick and the elderly.

Heat waves are particularly dangerous in urban areas because concrete, steel, asphalt, brick, and tar all reflect heat. In addition, there are fewer trees and less vegetation to absorb and cool the air. Heat builds up quickly and in the absence of wind forms a temperature inversion. An inversion layer traps the heat and prevents even small breezes from occurring. The air becomes stagnant, stifling. Individuals with breathing difficulty are at especially high risk during heat waves.

One of the most common mistakes that cost people their lives was keeping windows closed to avoid the heat from the outside. Temperatures were higher inside than they were outside, and there was no ventilation. Ventilation is critical, even if the temperature is warm. Another common mistake that resulted in many deaths was not drinking enough water. When overheated, the human body cools itself by producing sweat. If its reserve of water is depleted and not replenished the body becomes dehydrated and loses its ability to produce sweat, thus losing its ability to cool down. Those people who didn't drink enough water died of heat prostration, or heat stroke. Their bodies went into shock.

What should people do during a heat wave?

1. Drink plenty of water.
2. Wear a damp T-shirt.
3. Get near a breeze, or some type of moving air.
4. Reduce physical activity.
5. If possible, take frequent cool baths or showers.
6. Open windows at night.
7. Move to dark or shady parts of the house or building.
8. If possible, move to a lower floor.
9. Lie down on the floor if it is cooler.
10. Wear light cotton or minimal clothing.

Landslides

Topography, soil conditions, water content, and gravity are

important factors in determining the danger from landslides and avalanches. Those who live in mountainous or hilly areas, or in the foothills of mountain ranges need to be aware of the dangers of landslides and avalanches. As the population, and consequently the demand for housing, increases, land developers excavate and use hillsides for building sites. In most cases developers and contractors use the help from geologists to determine where and how houses can be built in a certain area. And for the most part developers scrape and pack the soil properly. Over time, however, weather conditions may be more severe than originally predicted. Land can erode more quickly or more severely than anticipated and create hazardous conditions.

The type of soil is also an important factor in determining how stable the land will be. Soil composed of sand, shale, or clay may be less stable than other types of soil. Even bedrock can have weaker zones in which fissures or bedding planes can create massive slides between different layers of soil. Water content is also significant. Because water levels rise and fall, soil can become saturated and, consequently, heavier and looser. Unusually heavy rainfall in any given area for an extended period of time will create slides. If rains are heavy over several seasons the groundwater could rise, which could eventually flow into fissures and create slides. If the ground freezes after a particularly wet season, the ice can push rocks apart and send the ground sliding. Some soils that don't drain well, such as clay, hold the water and send it sideways along the weakest points, which will also set the conditions for sliding.

The single most important factor that affects landslides, however, is gravity. Gravity pulls everything into its most comfortable state of rest. Over time, weather conditions, earthquakes, and commercial development can change the angle and support systems of any landscape. As those angles change, either through erosion or development, the underlying support for land masses may weaken.

For those living in a potential landslide area, it might be important to get a reliable geological survey every five years or so.

Avalanches

Snow avalanches follow many of the same basic dynamics of landslides, with one exception: snow can accumulate or diminish within a short period of time. The danger may not be visible until it is too late.

The presence of and relationship between four main factors determine the danger of an avalanche.

1. Critical mass. The critical mass of the snow means that the amount and density, and the weight of the snow is too much for the mountain to bear.
2. Layers. During accumulation, snow changes structurally. As snow builds up from one or more storms it creates different layers with varying densities, both hard and soft. Scientists believe that as snow builds up, it exerts pressure on the lower layers. With that pressure comes heat, which alters the form of the snow crystals. Lower levels eventually become warmer than surface levels, and the whole pack can begin to slide along the warmer level.
3. Slope. As with landslides, the angle of the slope is also critical. The problem is, the amount and type of snow can vary so much that it is hard to determine what will be a critical angle. Large amounts of wet snow can slide at angles smaller than fifteen degrees, while stable snow might stick to a slope of fifty degrees! So, while the slope is important, it is related to other factors as well.
4. Catalyst. There is always something that starts an avalanche. A large clump of snow falling from a peak, a sonic boom, a falling tree, a falling rock or ice mass, even a skier—all of these can trigger an avalanche if the conditions are right. When conditions are such that the potential for an avalanche is high, warnings are usually posted or officials will send out a team to release an avalanche through some aerial explosive.

Most frequently, skiers are the victims of avalanches. When caught in an avalanche, try to reach a tree, rock, or shrub to cling to. Hold on for dear life: the longer, the better. If swept away keep your mouth shut and use swimming motions to try to stay near the surface of the snow. As the avalanche slows, bring your arm in front of your mouth and nose to create some breathing space if you are buried. When everything is still, spit or dribble some saliva out of your mouth to determine which direction is down. Make one determined effort in the opposite direction to free yourself. If you cannot, remain still and try to stay calm so as to conserve your oxygen supply. If you have been skiing on the main slopes, it is likely you are not alone. Others will try to find you. If skiing the back peaks, however, wear a transceiver that puts out a signal in case you become lost.

Pestilence

Disasters that are caused by insects, animals, germs, and diseases fall under the category of pestilence. Locusts are well-known for their rapid reproduction in semiarid climate zones and their vast devastation of vegetation. They can wipe out hundreds of thousands of tons of crops in a very short period of time. They can bring famine and disease to an area. They multiply most quickly in the presence of drought. Regions of the Arabian Peninsula, the Sahara Desert, the Mediterranean coast, Australia, and the Great Plains of the United States have all had major outbreaks of locust.

With today's technology satellite pictures can determine when many of these areas are reaching the moisture condition that could promote rapid locust reproduction. Locust warnings are sent out and proper measure are taken to prevent such occurrences. There are, however, other forms of pestilence that have occurred.

Through intention or by accident, nonnative species have been introduced to foreign areas and have wreaked havoc. Through trade and travel, people have brought insects and diseases to other lands. One of the most famous examples is the Black Plague, which was brought to Europe in the 1340s. It killed nearly one-third of the population between India and Iceland. The Mexican fruit fly, the Asian cockroach, the gypsy moth, and the Colorado potato beetle are also examples of such accidental introductions that have wiped out crops in an area.

Thunderstorms

Thunderstorms result when warm moist air unites with cold air. Under normal conditions, the combination creates lightning, thunder, wind, and rain; in severe conditions, cyclones, hurricanes, and tornadoes can form. While thunderstorms occur in most parts of the world, the vast majority take place along the tropical zones of the planet where there is plenty of moisture and heat. More than one hundred thousand thunderstorms are reported annually in the United States alone. Damage from these storms can cost millions of dollars. Places such as Panama, Java, South America, Africa, the Gulf side of Mexico, and the Caribbean also have many thunderstorms each year. Strong winds can tear buildings apart, and the heavy rains can create flooding. But more often, severe damage is caused by the thunderstorm's counterpart: lightning.

Lightning Storms

Lightning is basically the discharge that occurs when oppositely charged electrical fields accumulate. Just how these charges build up and what determines a positive or negative charge is widely debated by scientists. Friction, freezing and melting, and temperature changes all seem to have some part in charging particles either negatively or positively. When opposite charges build up and come into contact with one another, the result is a powerful discharge of electrical energy that manifests in a lightning bolt.

Actually, a lightning bolt is a series of short bursts extending approximately fifty-five yards in length. This burst is followed by a very quick pause and then another burst. These bursts extend either from positive to negative, or from negative to positive. Once they have reached their target, they return along the same path. This is called the return stroke. Most lightning bolts consist of four leaders and their return strokes. Although this happens in stages, it is too quick for the human eye to see. It all happens within two-tenths of one second.

It is estimated that the temperature inside a lightning bolt is approximately 54,000 degrees Fahrenheit. The air around this lightning bolt heats so rapidly that it expands to the point of explosion, creating compression waves that produce thunder. People who are close to a lightning bolt hear thunder as a quick, sharp crack; those farther away hear it as a low, rolling sound with some reverberation.

Approximately one hundred people are struck and killed by lightning each year. Perhaps twice that amount are injured. The most common injuries are severe external and internal burns cause by the electricity. The severe jolts, however, can cause the stoppage of breath, cardiac arrest, and irregular heartbeats. Immediately applying CPR can reverse many of these effects.

When caught in a thunder or lightning storm, it is best to get inside a building or car. Never stand taller than anything in the surrounding area, and never stand next to a tree. The electrical current in lightning is drawn to the tallest object in the area of touchdown. And when it strikes the resulting shock wave can spread approximately three feet from the object struck. Never stand next to metal equipment, such as farming equipment or wire fences. And don't lay on the ground, since electrical current can run along the ground. If possible, find some dry clothes or a piece of rubber to sit on. These will act as insulators. If others are present, ask them to stay several yards apart. If in a car that is struck by lightning, wait at least a half an hour before exiting the car. Then, try to jump out without touching any metal parts. This will give the car time to dissipate its electrical charge.

Tidal Waves

Tidal waves occur most often in the Pacific Ocean and the Mediterranean Sea. They endanger many islands and coastal communities. Tidal waves, or tsunamis, as they are sometimes called, occur because of earthquakes, plate shifts, subaquatic landslides, and underwater volcanic eruptions. These large, underwater shifts can create huge waves that can travel hundreds of miles. Depending upon their distance from shore, and the topography of the ocean floor, some waves can hit land with a height of two hundred feet. While most tidal waves never reach this height, even waves of twenty to fifty feet can wipe out an entire coastal area.

Perhaps the most famous tidal wave came as a result of the volcanic eruption on the island of Krakatoa in August 1883. Krakatoa was located in the Sundra Strait, between the islands of Sumatra and Java. Smaller volcanic eruptions had been occurring in the area for three months before the volcano Rakata finally erupted in a massive explosion. Sea water rushed in to fill the partially emptied volcanic crater and created a huge explosion, sending a cloud of pulverized debris and steam high into the atmosphere. Tsunamis soon followed and completely overran the coastal lands of Sumatra and Java, killing more than thirty-six thousand people and destroying more than two hundred towns and villages. Reports from Merek, an area on the island of Java, estimated an average wave height of around 180 feet.

In 1946, because of a tidal wave that hit Hilo, Hawaii, the Pacific Tsunami Warning System was created. Today's satellite and computer technology can track seismic waves and can alert people when there is danger. But, like all warnings, people must heed them.

Transportation Disasters

Deaths from automobiles, motorcycles, airplanes, boats, and trains account for more deaths each year than all natural disasters combined. Most of the deaths result from driver or pilot error, which are usually caused by their being overly tired, reckless, under the influence of drugs or alcohol, or simply inexperienced. While no one can be completely safe wherever they are, heeding some of the following suggestions can greatly increase safety and the chance of survival.

1. Don't travel when the weather is bad. How much will it cost to be late? Is your life worth it?
2. Don't travel when the driver or pilot is tired, under the influence, or reckless.
3. Make sure the vehicle is in good operating condition. Any vehicle with torn, broken, rusted, or worn parts has probably not been well maintained.
4. Determine if the vehicle has safety and medical equipment aboard.

5. See if there are emergency instructions clearly visible on the vehicle. Taking one or two minutes to locate or ask someone about emergency measures is not too much to ask.

6. Traveling during the morning hours is usually safer than in afternoon and evening hours.

7. Restrict travel, if possible, from areas where there is obvious political and civil unrest.

Violent Crimes, Civil Disturbances, Riots, Bombings, and War

Conflict and aggression have been around since the beginning of time. They are everywhere—from the subatomic level to the highest forms of human existence. Like all creatures, human beings have a natural desire to live, receive attention, achieve, acquire, and protect their territory. The hope that human beings will be able to resolve their conflicts peacefully and channel their aggression constructively has also been around since the beginning of time. That ability, however, as most people can attest, is not yet universal. As the world population continues to grow, and natural resources diminish, fear and frustration are on the rise.

Whether the threat is real, or simply the effect of the media's focus on violence and crime, most people feel less safe in the world today. But going into hiding is neither appropriate nor possible. It is true, unfortunately, that car jackings, muggings, drive-by shootings, robbery, and rape are part of today's society. So are riots, racial and ethnic conflicts, and territorial disputes that involve hatred, violence, death, and destruction. Although some may consider themselves above violence and conflict, it is pervasive in many areas, and will likely continue to be so for some time to come. And it will likely affect every individual, sooner or later. There are several actions that can prepare people to handle physical violence.

1. Take the time to be aware of the immediate surroundings. Ask yourself the following questions:
   Am I vulnerable to an attack?
   Do I need to lock doors or windows?

Do I need to look at the people around me?

What would I do right now if someone tried to rape, rob, mug, or kidnap me?

How am I protecting myself right now from any one of these?

Where could I go right now for help?

What's would be a safer way to proceed?

By focusing on "right now," rather than sometime in the future, people can actually be prepared. Thirty seconds of awareness may be all it takes to save your life.

2. Play it safe. Don't go through risky parts of town. Don't stand out in a crowd unless it is safe to do so. Don't become an obvious target. Most people who are going about their routine—walking to and from their car, shopping, talking, driving, and so on—are focused on something other than their own safety. Consequently, they become prime targets. Plan ahead and play it safe. Remember, Las Vegas is wealthy because the odds are in its favor. People will stay safe by putting the odds in their favor.

3. Use the buddy system. It has been said, Two heads are better than one. This is especially true when it comes to matters of safety. Two people walking or riding in a car together is a much more formidable defense than a single individual walking or driving alone. Most violent crimes are committed by a single individual, on a single individual. If it is necessary to be out alone, however, let family members, friends, or co-workers know.

4. Take some instruction in personal safety or self-defense. Taking first-aid, CPR, personal safety, rape prevention, or martial arts classes is always a good step toward self-protection.

5. Know the environment. Take the time to know where the nearest hospital, fire department, and police station are. Find out if there are any stores that stay open late at night or all night. These places may be closer than other emergency facilities and may be able to call for help.

Drownings

It is easy to forget the inherent dangers water presents. A young child can drown in only a few inches of water. A bathtub, a wading pool, or even a shallow puddle can be a death trap for a small child. Swimming pools, lakes, ponds, creeks, rivers, wells, draining ditches—any body of water presents a potential drowning hazard. In rivers, lakes, and the ocean, however, there are the hidden dangers associated with tides and currents.

Most large-scale drownings result from floods, but from time to time, large ocean-going vessels and ferries sink, killing hundreds of people. Individual drownings are most frequently the result of recreational-boating and backyard swimming pool accidents. People are usually having fun and not paying attention to the potential danger and, in most cases, are not properly prepared for an accident. They have neither the skills nor the materials necessary to save the life of a drowning victim. The following are a few things that can prevent such disasters.

1. Take a class in CPR and first aid. Learn how to clear an air passage and resuscitate a drowning victim.
2. Take swimming lessons, and have children do the same as soon as they are able.
3. Make sure that children are supervised at all times if they are playing in or around water. A mother of two became a mother of one when she left her twin two-year-olds in a wading pool to take a phone call in the house.
4. Have and use proper water safety equipment such as life jackets, life rings, and life rafts.
5. Use the buddy system. Have at least one other person with you and/or let others know where you are going to be and when you will be back.
6. Don't use alcohol or drugs around water, and don't be around others who do.
7. Avoid reckless, risky, or dangerous behavior.
8. Don't go swimming in undesignated areas.
9. Know water safety laws when traveling by boat.
10. Don't travel on overcrowded boats. They will not have enough safety equipment and, most likely, will be unstable.

Toxic Spills

Human beings are truly their own worst enemies. With industrialization has come pollution. Materials toxic to the earth and its creatures have increased steadily, driven by ignorance, greed, and selfishness. At this point in history, mountains of hazardous waste fill the landscape—heaps that will take hundreds of thousands of years to be reabsorbed by the environment. This and other toxic waste pose a constant, tremendous threat to life.

Numerous industrial accidents have claimed thousand of lives over the years. One such accident took place in Bhopal, India in 1984. A chemical fertilizer plant sprung a major leak in one of its pipes, sending a huge toxic cloud into the early morning air. Many people in the neighboring town were still asleep as the searing gas created breathing difficulties and eventually destroyed people's lungs. Several thousand people died on that day alone.

Perhaps the nuclear accident at Chernobyl in the Soviet Union stands out as one of the worst industrial disasters in recent years. In the early morning hours of April 26, 1986, an explosion destroyed one of the plant's reactors, spewing several tons of uranium dioxide fuel and fission products into the air. Approximately one hundred sixteen thousand people were evacuated from the surrounding area. The toxic cloud endangered the lives of three to four hundred million people in neighboring countries. Rough estimates have suggested that at least twenty-four thousand people received a dose of radiation nearly double the maximum allowed in an entire lifetime. Only time will tell the true number of fatalities caused by that horrible accident.

Nearly every place on the planet has pollution of one form or another. The air, water, and earth are all connected. To pollute one is to pollute them all. With improvements in technology and heightened awareness of pollution and its true effects, there are an ever increasing number of things everyone can do to protect themselves, their families, and the environment.

1. Don't buy or use products that pollute. Learn which products are harmful to the environment, and which companies manufacture them.
2. Support legislation that protects the environment.

3. Have the air, land, and water inspected in the area, especially if moving into newly developed land.

4. Determine if any nearby factories or manufacturing plants use or produce toxic materials. Find out how and where they dispose of their waste. Learn the possible dangers of an explosion or spill. Where would the wind travel? Is the same ground water used? Plant and animal life, too, can carry toxins.

5. If there is no other option than to live near such a facility, check ground water and air periodically for unsafe levels of toxicity. If there is a potential for airborne toxins, consider having gas masks available for an emergency. Know how to use them and make sure that they are in good condition. Local fire departments will know where to get them.

15
The Media's Impact

Most people in this country watch television for one reason or another, whether for information, entertainment, or both. Many listen to the radio, and read newspapers and magazines as well. Overall, the media's impact is dramatic. It sensitizes people—that is, it alerts them to what is happening, often with horrific images of fires, floods, famine, and so on. When a disaster is approaching, especially one of massive proportion, continual media coverage can overload viewers, desensitizing them to what is happening. Use the media as a power tool of sorts, by controlling how, when, and for what it will be used. A disaster is not the time to use the television as a babysitter. The balance between getting information and upsetting a child's stability is an important one.

Your Family's Personality Makeup

Pause for a moment and consider the family's makeup. Do any family members—children or a spouse—upset easily? Does watching television disturb them? Do they believe that everything they see or hear may happen to them? Some people can watch television and act on the information presented without becoming upset. Others react to any and every possibility that something terrible is about to happen. Be especially careful with children. Some children are particularly sensitive to movies or stories they see on television. They may not say much at the time, but may later have nightmares, or difficulty sleeping or eating. They may become clinging and dependent out of fear that something might happen, either to them or to their parents.

Parents need to make a determination about how much they are going to allow the media to impinge upon the lives of their children. While watching or listening to the news can sometimes help them adopt a more realistic view of what is happening, the emotional impact can have damaging, long-range effects.

Using the Media for Information

Before a Disaster

Both television and radio have become the primary media for getting information quickly before a disaster. Newspapers and the Internet can also provide information, albeit less timely, about upcoming events. For example, hurricane, fire, earthquake, or flood watches and warnings help people prepare before a disaster strikes. Life-saving information about evacuation, road condition, shelters, first aid, special transportation, what to do, and when to do is also provided.

Most local agencies use the media to disseminate such information as quickly as possible. While national weather services and disaster agencies do their best, they are not always right. Sometimes the worst never comes to pass. Local news provides up-to-the-minute, accurate information, as the disaster is happening. Use of the news media is an essential part of disaster preparation.

Parents should be cautious, however. While television provides critical information about what to expect and how to prepare for disasters, care and sensitivity must be exercised. While preparing for a disaster, particularly weather-related disasters, there is a tendency for the entire family to watch the television closely. Some family members will become desensitized to what they are seeing. By watching too many disastrous events on the news, people can start to believe that disasters always happen somewhere else, and to other people. They can become complacent, believing it will never happen to them, and thus, not realize or believe in the importance of being prepared. Others may not be able to watch without becoming unduly alarmed. Whatever their family's reaction, parents must make the decision to stop viewing the coverage, or simply to watch it themselves.

During a Disaster

It is during a disaster that proper use of media coverage can be especially important. First of all, information about what to do and where to go for specific help is essential. The location of safety shelters is different for different disasters. In earthquakes, for example, shelters are typically located in buildings that are protected from earthquake damage; in floods, they are on high ground. And sometimes, shelters can be relocated during severe disasters in which the damage is more than expected. Always keep a battery-operated, portable television or radio on hand to stay in touch with what is happening. Information is a powerful tool. Used correctly, it can save lives.

After a Disaster

After a period of time, as the actual disaster passes, people can begin to think about getting assistance, if necessary, and putting their lives back together. Once a disaster has struck, the media usually provides directions to and information about emergency services available, as well as the future course, if any, of the disaster and the extent of damage to surrounding areas. While this information is useful for those who are ready to get on with their lives, some people may still be in shock from the traumatic event. These people, in particular, may be disturbed by the interminable media coverage that typically follows a disaster. Viewing continuous scenes of damage and destruction on television, or hearing about the event over and over can be reinforcing, and actually worsen their trauma. In severe cases of shock or trauma, perpetual reinforcement of the disaster can slow, or even impede, their recovery. It is very important for parents to determine what is best for each individual member of the family. Controlling others' use of the media can be especially difficult, however, if parents themselves are watching television or listening to disaster coverage continuously.

What to Do

The media is a double-edged sword. Obtaining the information it provides may be absolutely essential to the welfare of the family; however, constant viewing and reinforcement of a traumatic time may be harmful. The question is what to do when a disaster occurs.

Ideally, parents should decide the amount of media coverage necessary for their family's education and survival. If the images or descriptions seem to be disturbing for children, parents should limit viewing times. Parents should also consider their own reaction to continual disaster coverage. Watching repetitious scenes of destruction is not healthy or helpful for them either. Use the media judiciously; do not let it overwhelm.

The Nature of the Media

Because television is the most popular method of getting information today, it is important to understand how news programs operate. Each station tries to make its news programs more popular that any other. To do this, stations present the most dramatic and interesting stories and footage available. They study the demographics of their audience, and often slant their stories to appeal to that audience. Television stations are interested in presenting correct and accurate information, but the time they allot to ordinary events or stories is often minimal.

In the interest of public safety, however, even when the information may be considered tedious, television stations are extremely responsible about reporting what to do and where to get help. Many would say that this information is presented because the context in which it is offered creates the dramatic excitement television stations covet. While such a theory is certainly plausible, it does little to circumvent the fact that critical, and often life-saving, information is provided by television stations during a crisis, and society should be thankful that such up-to-the-minute, accurate assistance is available.

Other Media

There are several videos available about how to prepare for and what to do during disasters. They can be valuable for alerting family members what to expect, and thinking through preparation measures. But parents should be cautious in allowing children or particularly sensitive adults to view such videos. The images are usually extremely graphic, and can easily frighten some people.

16

The Aftereffects— Years after a Disaster

Many people have short memories, particularly of unpleasant events. Disasters can often leave their mark, however, even when people are unaware of what is happening to them. Those that suffer severe emotional injuries may be unable to forget. For most people who survive a disaster, the memories are good, or a mixture of good and bad, with the bad fading over time. The following sections look at some long-term aftereffects of disaster, both positive and negative.

Positive Aftereffects

Life experiences change everyone. Disaster survivors, if they do not suffer major trauma or loss, often change in the direction of becoming stronger and more self-reliant. When they look back five years after a disaster, most people say that the event left them more cautious, more protective of their family, and much better prepared, at least in terms of preventing emotional trauma. Many hold practice drills every few months, so that every family member will know what their role is if an emergency happens. These drills create a sense of control, which leads to feeling greater self-confidence and being better prepared, and thus, having a better chance of survival.

Also, the very fact that people planned and prepared effectively, did the right thing, and performed their assigned role correctly can leave them with a feeling of self-confidence that they will be able to react positively in any stressful situation.

Some families carry this confidence and preparedness to their communities, organizing self-help groups and neighborhood alliances. Although they may not be enough in large-scale, widespread disasters, such community groups are the wave of the future in disaster preparation and relief. These help groups can be particularly helpful in a large disaster when there are not enough emergency services available. Ambulances and paramedics, for example, can be spread awfully thin when 300 people are calling for assistance. Small communities working together may be the best first line of defense in a major disaster. Working together as a community can also bring individual families closer together, adding a sense of belonging and a collective stake in the future. These types of alliances tend to be more common in rural areas, but are springing up in cities across the country.

Many people find that after a disaster their values begin to change. They often become more spiritual, and more family- and community-oriented. They are thankful they have endured the threat of possible loss and survived, and are more careful and loving with the people in their life.

Just as war veterans form a bond at having suffered and survived together, survivors and emergency workers also bond during and after a disaster. When thrown together under extreme conditions, people learn to trust and respect one another, regardless of cultural and other differences. Going through such an event brings out the goodness in people, and often creates mutual feelings of hope, faith, thankfulness, admiration, and sometimes love. The emotional and physical pain people experience in a disaster becomes a permanent part of their lives. And sometimes, those who have gone through it with them become life-long friends.

Negative Aftereffects

Disasters bring their share of tragedy and horror. Losing a home, and a lifetime of plans and hard work can be tragic. Losing a loved one or seeing a child hurt may be one of life's most painful events.

Everyone expects to feel anxious during and immediately after a disaster, but what if that anxiety does not disappear? Posttraumatic stress is a real problem—a problem that requires professional help. The difficulty with such emotional aftermath is that it does not always show itself immediately, nor is it always obvious. Sometimes people experience delayed reactions that can have long-term effects. A child who tries to be "good" by not burdening his or her parents with feelings of fear, or an adult who keeps a stiff upper lip by holding his or her feelings in, may seem fine initially, just a little quiet. Years later, however, these individuals may find that they have changed. Such changes can put an enormous strain on people, as well as on their relationships, partly because they are unconscious changes. They may be manifest themselves in a difficulty in trusting what is going to happen, or may even border on paranoia. These people may never be able to relax completely, staying in a constant state of vigilance, always ready for the worst to happen. They may forever carry a sense of guilt with them, for what they did or did not do at the time of the disaster.

No one is certain how long delayed reactions take to surface. For most people, these feelings surface within a year. But for others, feelings linger in the subconscious, only to surface when some trigger releases them. News of a similar disaster, a familiar smell, or even the sound of a child crying—triggers do not have to be logical. Frequently, they are not. When repressed feelings resurface, they are usually just as powerful as they were initially.

They can be terrifying, painful, and may interfere with a person's life to the same extent as they would if the event had occurred yesterday.

Rarely do all members of a family feel or react the same way after a disaster. Fathers and mothers may have different priorities. Boys and girls may react differently, depending upon how they perceive their role in the family. Older children typically react differently that their younger siblings. Personality, as well as life experience determine how they feel and what they do. Although five years is a long time, some people may not be able to let go of the fear they felt, or the horror of what they saw and heard. This group constitutes a small percentage of the population, but it is one that everyone needs to be aware of. As survivors of earthquakes, we, the authors, still tense up when a heavy truck goes by and shakes the building we are in.

Families, Years Later

How did the families mentioned earlier in this book fare?

Henry Northcutt, his wife, Julie, and their three children still live in Texas. Both Henry and Julie have completely recovered from the flood's damage and the emotional turmoil it caused. Their commitment to being prepared keeps them in a constant state of readiness for almost any disaster. They see disasters as part of the natural flow of life. Floods, droughts, bad years, good years—all are taken in stride. Their daughter, Theresa, however, still suffers from nightmares, though they are becoming less and less frequent with time. When Theresa had gone to retrieve a calf that was stuck in a muddy field and had gotten stuck, she truly believed she was going to die. The water was rising, the calf was squealing, and Theresa was yelling, all to no avail. When her father had finally come to rescue her, there was not enough time to rescue the calf, which was later drowned.

Theresa was never able to forget that calf. She felt somehow responsible for its death although she knew she could not have done anything else to save it. She also felt guilty that she had survived and the calf had not. For a young child—she was six at the time—attachment to animals can be powerful. The Northcutts eventually took Theresa to a counselor, who continues to help her let go of her feelings. After one year of professional help, Theresa is beginning to put the incident behind her. What remains is an acute awareness of what floods can do, and an intense feeling of responsibility for those she cares about.

Joanne Rodriguez and her two daughters, Rosa and Maria, moved out of the apartment building to a small house. The children recovered quickly from the earthquake. Even Rosa, who took longer to recover, no longer worries about earthquakes. Joanne, who had been through an earthquake in Mexico in which she lost a brother, as well as the earthquake in California, was filled with a persistent anxiety after the incident. Whether caused by a passing or a mild aftershock, whenever she felt a shake her heart began to beat faster. Few pictures are hung on the walls of her new home; those that are, are covered in plastic, rather than glass. All the furniture is bolted to the floor and walls, and she has emergency lights in every room and keeps a crowbar in her bedroom. She is ready for the next quake, and is sure it is coming. Her fear does not encompass only earthquakes, however. Joanne is always concerned—usually overly concerned—for the safety of her daughters, particularly Rosa, whom she almost lost. Joanne functions fairly well in her normal routine, until she feels something shake. In an instant, her memories come flooding back, including the terror she felt during the earthquake in Mexico. She is currently preparing to move to an area that has no earthquakes.

Chris and Mary Byron and their three children, Mark, Elliott, and Joan, were also involved in the earthquake in Northridge, California. Both adequate preparation and early professional intervention for the children seems to have taken care of most of the problems. Chris and Mary feel strong and self-confident that they endured and survived such an enormous disaster. Mark and Elliott have already overcome their anxiety and are doing well in school. Joan, the youngest, has finally begun to sleep alone in her own room. She feels anxious occasionally, especially when there is a mild quake or if she hears loud or strange noises. In these instances, she still rushes into her parents' room. Chris and Mary usually hold her for a while and reassure her that everything is all right. When she begins to relax again, she returns to her own room. Joan no longer requires a night-light in her room, but always wants the hall light left on and her door open. Both Chris and Mary feel comfortable with Joan's progress. They feel that she is getting stronger as time passes. They are prepared, however, if Joan stops making progress, to bring her back to the psychologist for further help.

Henry and Marge Wilson still live in the same house, now repaired and structurally better able to withstand hurricanes. Their children, Mark and Helen, are fine, although they sense their parents' anxiety during every hurricane season. Henry sees each hurricane season as an opportunity to beat Mother Nature. Marge is less concerned with victory; her worry is about the children's welfare. Whenever a hurricane watch is called, she begins to pack the car for a trip to her parents' house. While Henry usually argues that there is no reason to leave, Marge remains determined. They frequently argue, and then they prepare to leave. They have taken measures to protect their home against water and strong winds, as much as they are able to protect it. Outside trees are kept trimmed and anything moveable is put away or secured adequately for the worst of winds. They are well prepared for the next disaster. They have not been able to resolve their philosophical differences about hurricanes, but Marge is adamant about evacuating early, and she usually wins. She will, for a short time, watch the news with Henry, hoping for the direction of the hurricane to change, but when her anxiety becomes too great she loads the kids into the car. Henry usually wants to stay, but gives in begrudgingly and drives the family to his parents' house.

Marge Woosterman had not changed. She now knows the area better, and, having survived a fire unscathed, feels less anxious about fires. When the fire had threatened her and her son, David, they both knew the drill. They had taken the necessary precautions advised by forest rangers to protect their home, and had kept the necessary supplies ready. Their primary concern is the safety of their pets. Leaving one cat behind when they evacuated left them anxious for the next time. David, in particular, worried about the pets he had grown up with. He knew he would be terribly upset if he lost one in a fire. At the first sign of difficulty, he gathers them all into the house and immediately puts the most difficult cats into a carrying cage. He feels he would rather be too safe than lose one, especially in a fire. Today he respects fires more than he did, but feels more in control now that he is better prepared. Marge sees how frightened David is about losing a pet, but thinks his anxiety is under control, as long as it isn't affecting him too much in everyday life.

The final family, the Simpsons, are also faring quite well, considering the enormity of the crisis they experienced. Evan Simpson still runs his pharmacy and Shirley continues to take care of the home and volunteers at her church. Evan Jr., who was shot in the leg, has almost totally recovered. A slight limp persists, but it is almost unnoticeable. He is not able to participate in certain sports, which bothers him somewhat, but, as a bright and imaginative boy, he is able to fill his time with many other enjoyable activities, such as using his computer. Gloria, now twelve, has not fared quite as well. She had been in and out of treatment for the last five years. Although they are less frequent now, she had recurring nightmares after the incident of somebody coming into her room and hurting her. The event left a marked impression on her that she couldn't let go. While Evan and Shirley relied on their faith and the church to help them, and Evan Jr. had his computer and his friends, Gloria experienced difficulties both with friends and with schoolwork. Her parents believe she is not a bad girl, just one who spends too much time daydreaming. Gloria had, and still has, a number of problems to resolve. She continues to work through them.

Overall, these families fared remarkably well. Those that were prepared fared the best. The message is clear: Families that educate themselves about disasters and prepare with appropriate materials do better than those who do not. Families that involve themselves with their local community, whether a large apartment house, or one or more city blocks, do better than those who do not. It is up to you, as parents, how well your family will fare. Start preparing now.

Appendix A

Materials to Purchase at Camping or Emergency Supply Stores

1. Dried, packaged food and/or food bars
2. Water purifiers
3. Water carriers
4. Packaged water
5. Survival bag, or multi-use sleeping bag
6. Tube tent of heavy-duty vinyl, large enough for two people
7. First-aid kit
8. Hand warmers
9. Vials to hold various medications
10. Thermometer, in a plastic case
11. Portable radio with batteries, or solar/dynamo radio with four different power sources
12. Flashlight
13. Candle lantern and candles
14. Duct tape, or all-purpose tape for weather proofing, covering broken windows, or other repairs
15. Crowbar
16. Folding shovel
17. Camper saw
18. Backpacker's stove or Sterno stove
19. Backpack, to be carried in your car
20. Manual can opener
21. Plastic plates, cups, knives, forks, and spoons
22. Camper's cooking set
23. Cover, tarp, or other emergency shelter
24. Emergency tool to turn off gas, water, electricity, or other tools

Appendix B

A Pre- or Posttrauma Relaxation Tape

First Stage

Read this section into a tape recorder, and listen to it when you need to. The technique herein is designed to teach you not only how to relax, but how to relax quickly. Initially, it takes thirty minutes to learn the technique. Continued practice will allow you to relax more quickly, eventually, in as little as one minute. This technique goes beyond relaxing during a disaster, however, it is extremely effective for reducing everyday stress and anxiety.

Allow thirty minutes for the exercise. Sit in a comfortable chair or on a couch, with your head and neck supported. Loosen or remove any restrictive clothing that may become uncomfortable as you relax. Uncross your arms and legs, and place your feet flat on the floor. Take several deep breaths, breathing in and releasing each breath slowly. Notice how each exhalation relaxes you slightly more. Feel yourself sink into the chair. As you start to relax, let all your tension go.

Take a deep breath, and hold it to the count of four; 1, 2, 3, 4. Let it out slowly, to the count of eight; 1, 2, 3, 4, 5, 6, 7, 8. Now hold it, without taking another breath; 1, 2, 3, 4. Notice how your breathing begins to slow down. Breathe in; 1, 2, 3, 4. Breathe out; 1, 2, 3, 4, 5, 6, 7, 8. Hold it; 1, 2, 3, 4. (The exact numbers are not as important as the natural rhythm you develop. Establish your own pace, and repeat this exercise to your own count.)

After a minute or two, stop counting. Notice how easy, comfortable, and warm you feel, as you begin to relax. Continue this breathing through the second stage of relaxation.

Second Stage

As you continue to breathe, begin to relax your muscles. Release any tension in your body. Imagine your tension flowing from the top of your head, all the way down your body and out your toes, as if gravity was pulling the tension out of you. Check your forehead, around your eyes and ears, your nose, the back of your head, your mouth, your chin, and the skin of your face. Let the tension flow downward, so you feel fully relaxed, warm, and comfortable. Check your neck and shoulders, release the tension, letting it flow down. Check your arms, wrists, hands, and fingers, letting the tension flow out of the tips of your fingers. Check your chest, back, stomach, hips, thighs, knees, calves, down to your ankles, letting the tension flow downward. Now imagine all that tension in your feet. Breathe in; 1, 2, 3, 4. Breathe out; 1, 2, 3, 4, 5, 6, 7, 8, letting the tension flow through your toes and out of your body. Feel how relaxed your body is. Continue to breathe, deeply, comfortably. If any area of your body is holding onto some tension, return to that area and let the tension go. (As you practice, notice how quickly you can relax, and how marvelous you feel being fully relaxed.)

Let the tension escape. Breathe in, 1, 2, 3, 4; and out, 1, 2, 3, 4, 5, 6, 7, 8. Keep checking your body for tension, relaxing ever more deeply as you let it go. (The actual, physical feeling may vary. You may feel heavier and heavier, as you sink into the chair, or you may have a feeling of lightness, as the tension leaves your body. Some areas of your body can be relaxed easily; others will take more work and repeated practice.)

Notice how your body feels as it begins to relax. Continue the deep breathing, continue to check the different parts of your body, letting all the tension go. Notice how good you feel as the tension leaves you, how much better and more comfortable your body feels.

Third Stage

Notice how your mind wanders as you try to relax, how it jumps from the important to the unimportant. (It's extremely difficult to clear your mind completely, to think of nothing at all. Try to keep your mind as clear as possible, but don't fight sporadic thoughts.

Don't try not to think of something, just let your mind think it and then let it go, feeling ever more comfortable and relaxed. If you don't fight them, thoughts go away on their own accord. The next few sentences may help you keep your mind clear.) Focus on your breathing. Feel your stomach going up and down, as you inhale and exhale. Feel the air passing over your upper lip, as the cool air enters and exits your nose.

(As you learn to focus on one thing at a time, you'll find that as you repeat these exercises, your thinking and your thoughts tend not to bother you as much. You'll find that you feel more and more relaxed and your thoughts are clearer and clearer. It helps to become one with your concentration. Concentrate on your breathing and nothing else. If other thoughts come into your mind, let them go. The most important thing is to feel fully relaxed and very comfortable, with your mind at rest, as much as possible.) You now feel very relaxed and very comfortable. There are no problems that need to be solved at this moment. Relaxation is taking over your body. Now, check your breathing again. Breath in, 1, 2, 3, 4; and out, 1, 2, 3, 4, 5, 6, 7, 8. Keep yourself fully relaxed, feel comfortable. Check the tension in your body. Where is there still tension? Breathe in as you concentrate on those areas, and out as you let the tension go.

Notice how you feel sleepier and sleepier as you relax; feeling warmer and very comfortable. Use the sounds in the room, whatever they may be. A clock ticking, noises in the other room, people talking—use these sounds to help you relax.

Notice how good you are beginning to feel as you relax, very comfortable and very relaxed, going deeper and deeper into a state of relaxation and comfort. See yourself riding down an escalator. Notice the feeling of gravity, the motion, the feel of the handrail as you put your hand on it to steady yourself. The further down you go, the deeper and more relaxed you feel. Know that you are always in control; you can step off the escalator at any point. You can always ride the up escalator to return to the present. You are in control.

Take a few minutes to relax on your own, (pause the tape) without any suggestions, feeling more and more comfortable, very relaxed. (As you practice, silence will become easier.) Become totally relaxed and very comfortable, not worrying about anything, not thinking about anything, just being relaxed. Notice how it feels to be relaxed, how comfortable, how warm, how good it feels. You can become active whenever you want to be, since you are in control. For now, relax and be comfortable. Notice how good it feels, very relaxed, very comfortable, very relaxed, very comfortable. Check the tension in your body. Are all parts of your body relaxed? If not, breathe into them, breathing deeper and deeper, more and more comfortable. Resist the impulse to get up and do something; just relax. It is easy for you to do many things. It is easy for you to do many things at one time. It is very difficult for you to do nothing at all. Just relax. Rest your body and mind; allow your unconscious to take over. Let thoughts that need to come out escape. Achieving that sense of calmness, focusing on one thing at a time, is essential. Just relax yourself.

Feeling yourself relaxed, go deeper and deeper into that state of relaxation. You're very, very comfortable, and able to come back to the present whenever you wish, since you are in control. For the present, you're choosing to feel very relaxed, very comfortable, breathing into those areas of tension, clearing your mind, just feeling good, very relaxed. Just breathe deeply; reach a new level of relaxation. (You will find that once you've reached a certain level of relaxation, there is always a level below that.) Feeling very relaxed and comfortable, very relaxed, very comfortable. Check your body from time to time, make sure you're comfortable where you are sitting. Make sure your body is supported. As you relax and keep your mind clear, you will find new sensations, new sensitivities to sights, sounds. Your body is becoming more in tune to what is around it, breathing deeply, feeling very relaxed and very comfortable, very relaxed. Notice how peaceful you feel, how totally relaxed, centered. Notice how the deep breathing helps you focus your mind and keep it clear, feeling very relaxed and very comfortable.

For the final few minutes, try to go even deeper into a relaxed state, becoming more comfortable, more relaxed. Check your breathing. Notice how with each breath you become more relaxed. Notice as you breath into those areas of your body that are still tense, they become more relaxed. Feel your mind relax with your body. Notice how comfortable you feel, how care seems to drift away, just being totally relaxed. Now, just sit there for the next few minutes, continuing to breathe and relax.

Slowly bring yourself back to the present, feeling energized, comfortable, and in total control of your body.

Try this method during the day, whenever you have a few minutes to spare. You will need to practice continuously, on a daily basis, if possible, until you can bring yourself to a relaxed state quickly and effectively.

If you would like a copy of the preceding relaxation exercise on tape, please call or write to:

The Learning Center
16944 Ventura Blvd
Encino, CA 91316
(818) 783-6633

Bibliography

Ebert, Charles, H. V. *Disasters*. Dubuque: Kendall Hunt Publishing Co., 1988.

Farberow, Norman L. and Norma S. Gordon. *Manual for Child Health Workers in Major Disasters*. Washington, D.C.: National Institute of Mental Health, 1986.

Johnson, Kendall. *Trauma in the Lives of Children*. Claremont, Calif.: Hunter House, Inc., 1945.

Johnson, Kendall. School Crisis Management. Alameda, Calif.: Hunter House, Inc., 1993.

Kimball, Virginia. *Earthquake Ready*. Santa Monica: Roundtable Publishing, Inc., 1988.

Lane, Frank W. *The Violent Earth*. Topsfield, Mass.: Salem House, 1986.

Lystad, Mary, ed. *Innovations in Mental Health Services to Disaster Victims*. Rockville, Md.: National Institute of Mental Health, 1985.

Mitchell, Jeffrey T. and Grady Bray. *Emergency Services Stress*. Englewood Cliffs, N.J.: Prentice-Hall, Inc., 1990.

Mitchell, Jeffrey T. and George S. Everly Jr. *Critical Incident Stress Debriefing*. Ellicott City, Md.: Chevron Publishing Corp., 1995.

Everly Jr., George S. and Jeffrey M. Lating, eds. *Psychotraumatology: Discussing the Results of Disasters Such As Posttraumatic Stress*. New York: Plenum Press, 1995.

Santa Clara County Department of Health, "Earthquakes: A Survival Guide for Seniors" Santa Clara County, Calif.: Department of Health, 1991.

Saylor, Conway F., ed. *Children and Disasters*. New York: Plenum Press, 1993.

Tierney, Kathleen J. and Barbara Baisden. *Crisis Intervention Programs for Disaster Victims.* Rockville, Md.: National Institute of Mental Health, 1979.

Index

acute stress disorder, 10–11, 76

adolescents, 112

aftereffects, 62, 77, 101, 153, 155, 157, 159

aftershocks, 85

American Red Cross, 100, 102–3, 122

avalanches, 135–36

beepers, 52

blizzards, 129–30

bombings, 1, 141–42

CB radios, 53, 69

cellular telephones, 52

Chronic Posttraumatic Stress Disorder, 10–11, 77

climate, 27, 42, 137

cold spells, 129–30

Critical Incident Stress Management, 122

crown fires, 132

cyclones, 125, 138

depression, 2, 6, 9, 23, 74, 78, 89–90, 110

disorientation, 9, 64, 110

drought, 28, 105, 130–31, 137

drownings, 143

earthquakes, 1, 4, 26–27, 37, 56, 63–64, 74, 85, 128, 135, 139, 149, 156–57, 169

elderly, 13–14, 43, 46, 56, 86, 109–12, 129, 134

explosions, 1, 128

Federal Emergency Management Agency, 101

fires, 1, 4, 26–27, 51, 53, 55–56, 63–64, 105–6, 128, 131–33, 147, 158

flashbacks, 11, 23, 72, 77

floods, 1, 4, 26–28, 51, 55, 124, 127–28, 143, 147, 149, 156–57

ground fires, 131–32

handicapped, 13–14, 86, 109, 112

Hans Selye, 7

heat waves, 133–34

hurricanes, 1, 4, 27–28, 51, 55–56, 74, 81–82, 85, 125–26, 138, 158

hypothermia, 44, 53–54, 129–30

impaired cognitive functioning, 27
insomnia, 3
International Critical Incident
Stress Foundation, ix

landslides, 63–64, 134–36,
139
lightning storms, 138–39

mass fires, 132
media, 69, 73, 86, 126–27,
141, 147–51

Neighborhood Watch, 47
nightmares, 3, 18, 22, 27, 67,
122, 148, 156, 159
numbness, 9–10, 23, 73, 76
nutrition, 78

personality, 2, 10, 12, 14–15,
76, 93, 96, 115, 147, 156
pestilence, 137
physical fitness, 38
play, 3, 25–26, 32, 41–42, 45,
64, 67, 73, 78, 89–90, 94,
96–97, 107, 119, 126, 142
posttraumatic stress, 2, 6,
10–11, 15, 72, 76–77,
102–3, 155, 169
Posttraumatic Stress Disorder,
10–11, 77
prayer, 67
psychosomatic disease, 7

radio, 54–56, 59, 69–70, 75,

82, 86, 123–28, 147–49,
161
rape, 1, 3, 120, 141–42
Red Cross, 3, 13, 52, 87,
100–3, 107, 117, 122, 124,
126–27
regression, 9, 18, 21
rehabilitation, 96
riots, 141–42
rituals, 79, 90
routines, 22–24, 70, 73, 79,
89

Salvation Army, 100
shelters, 3–4, 48, 52, 69, 91,
100–101, 116–17, 126,
148–49
shock, 7, 9, 11, 36, 61–62, 65,
71–74, 76–77, 103, 134,
139, 149–50
shootings, 1, 4, 141
sleep, 3, 18–19, 44–45, 62,
77, 87, 90, 95, 97, 107,
110, 116–17, 157
stress, 2–3, 6–11, 13, 15, 18,
20–21, 66, 72, 76–78, 90,
92, 96, 100, 102–3, 115,
117, 121–22, 130, 155,
163, 169
stressor, 7
surface fires, 131

television, 5, 19, 25, 32, 36,
39, 68–70, 75, 82–83, 86,
97, 106–7, 123–24,
126–28, 147–51

terrorism, 1

thunderstorms, 27, 123, 138

tidal waves, 139–40

tornadoes, 4, 26–27, 30, 51, 56, 123–24, 138

toxic spills, 144–45

transportation disasters, 140–41

trauma, 3, 6, 14, 16, 23, 87–88, 102–3, 150, 154, 169

tsunamis, 139–40

typhoons, 125

volcanoes, 124–25

war. 141–42

Your Own Disaster Plan

Disasters Known to Strike My Area of the Country

_____

_____

_____

_____

_____

_____

_____

_____

_____

_____

_____

_____

Emergency Supplies My Family Will Need

_____

_____

_____

_____

_____

_____

_____

_____

_____

_____

_____

_____

_____

_____